# the *Animated* JEWISH YEAR

Written by
**Danny Wool & Yefim (Chaim) Yudin**

Illustrations
**Inbal Beter & Jeremy Portnoi**

# The Animated Jewish Year

Written by **Danny Wool** & **Yefim (Chaim) Yudin**
Art director and photographer: **Jeremy Portnoi**
Clay models: **Inbal Beter**
Additional clay models: **Liz Blazer**
Additional photography: **Shelly Elish**
Graphic design: **Stephanie & Ruti Design**
Cover design: **Judy & Claudia Graphic Design**
Calendar design: **Jeremy Portnoi & Liz Blazer**
Consultant: Robert Binder
Editors:
**Dr. Seymour Epstein**
**Shoshana Kligman**
**Jonathan Lubell**
**Pamela Feldman**
**Naomi Schacter**

Printed and bound by **Keterpress Enterprises**, Jerusalem

ISBN 965-7108-79-9

Produced by: **Scopus**

Published and distributed by: **Lambda Publishers Inc.**
3709 13th Ave., Brooklyn, NY 11218, USA
Tel: (718)972-5449 | Fax: (718)972-6307 | e-mail: animatedjewishyear@ejudaica.com
www.lambdapublishers.com | www.UrimPublications.com

Distributed in Israel by: **Urim Publications**
P.O.Box 52287, Jerusalem 91521 Israel
Tel: 02-679-7633 | Fax: 02-679-7634 | e-mail: Animated@UrimPublications.com | www.UrimPublications.com

Distributed in England by: **Judaica World**
2-4 Kings Road, Prestwich, Manchester, M25 OLE, United Kingdom | Tel: +44 161 773 4956 | email: boaz76@aol.com

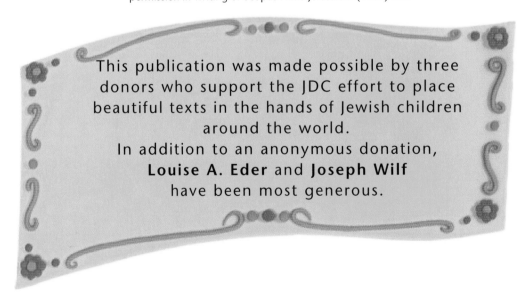

This publication was made possible by three
donors who support the JDC effort to place
beautiful texts in the hands of Jewish children
around the world.
In addition to an anonymous donation,
**Louise A. Eder** and **Joseph Wilf**
have been most generous.

# Introduction

If the previous volume, *The Shabbat Book*, was meant to introduce Jewish children to Jewish time, this book is designed to explore that time in all of its historical, cultural, ethical, literary and spiritual elements.

The first steps were taken by introducing the Jewish week, in which the Torah portion provides us with a weekly narrative of legend and law, that culminates in the glorious palace we call Shabbat.

Now, in this book, we chart the entire calendar to provide the knowledge, feelings, and internal thoughts surrounding each and every holy day of the Jewish year. The ultimate goal of this book is to put aside the months we know best, January through December, and to learn the rhythm of our own Hebrew months, Tishrei through Elul.

Chaim Nachman Bialik, the national Jewish poet of this century, once wrote an essay to justify the celebration of Chanukah as a national event, aside from any spiritual significance the holiday has for believing Jews. In that brief essay, he uses a metaphor for the holidays of Israel with which all Jews can identify. He compares our holidays, happy and sad, to mountains in time that testify to earlier volcanic eruptions and earthquakes in our history. These were cataclysmic events so powerful at the time that they left indelible records in the annals of our people. As we traverse these "mountains" each year they bring us back to earlier events in our formative years as a people. On the way, we note lesser hills that testify to other dramatic moments in our history, similar in nature and just as significant for those who lived the actual experience.

Since Bialik's writing, we have written new chapters in our history and set aside special days to commemorate these events as well. The generations of the future will see new mountains, where we actually lived the horrors of the Holocaust, the pride of the establishment of the State of Israel, the tragic loss of Israeli soldiers, and the joy of the reunification of Jerusalem, our capital. Yom HaSho'ah VehaGevurah, Yom Ha'Atzma'ut, Yom HaZikaron, and Yom Yerushalayim are, by now, part of our calendar landscape.

This book is dedicated to the "new Jews" of the Former Soviet Union who have come back to the Jewish people after a long spiritual separation. The Russian edition was written for their children in a language they can understand so that, eventually, our holidays will be theirs and our language theirs: our customs of joy and suffering shared by Jews equally all over the world.

*Dr. Seymour Epstein*
*Director of Jewish Education*
*American Jewish Joint Distribution Committee*

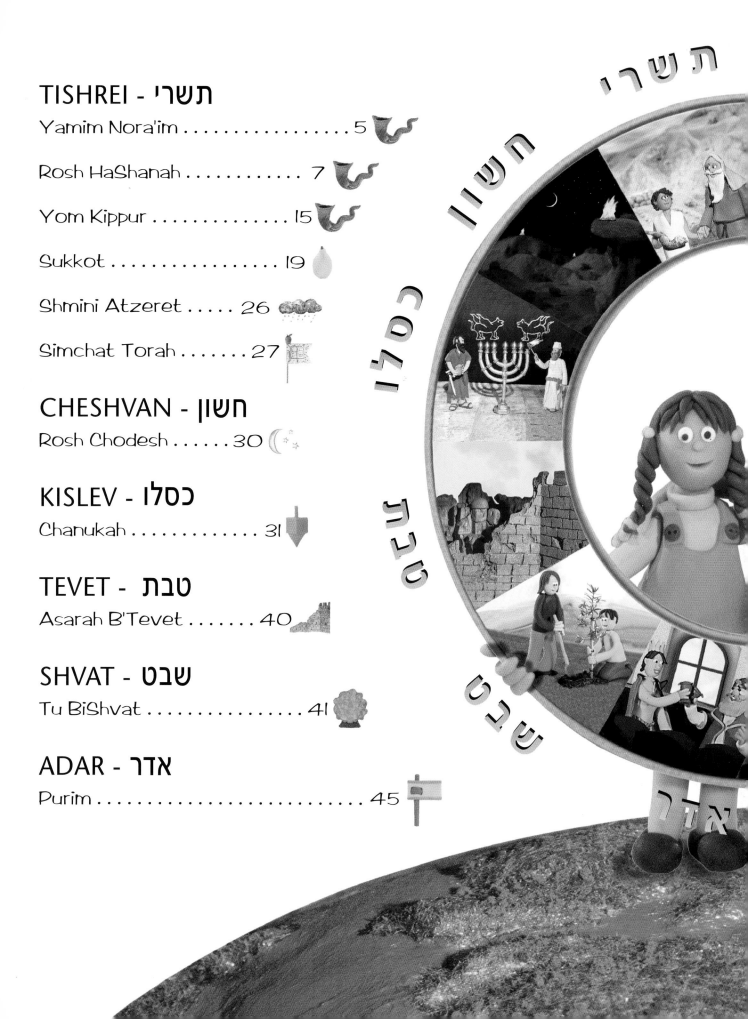

**Marcy:** Hi there, you must be the new boy in school.

**Max:** Yes, I am.

**Marcy:** What's your name?

**Max:** Max. What's yours?

**Marcy:** I'm Marcy. Have you ever studied in a Jewish school before?

**Max:** No, never, but my parents want me to know more about being Jewish. They're even talking about moving to Israel one day.

**Marcy:** You must be so excited. My family is going to make aliyah at the end of the year.

**Max:** What are they going to make? You'll have to start using words I understand.

**Marcy:** Aliyah, that's Hebrew for moving to Israel.

**Max:** Wow! I didn't even start school and I already know some Hebrew. What else do you study here?

**Marcy:** This year we're going to learn all about the Jewish holidays.

**Max:** Jewish holidays? Are there a lot?

**Marcy:** There certainly are. There's a holiday almost every month.

**Max:** Wow! Holidays mean no school.

**Marcy:** Well, it's not exactly like that. There's a lot to do on these holidays.

**Max:** Homework?

**Marcy:** Not exactly homework. All the <u>chagim</u> - that's Hebrew for holidays - have their own <u>minhagim</u> - things we do to make the holiday special. There are special foods, stories, songs, parties...

**Max:** Food? Stories? Parties? I like this kind of homework. When do we start?

**Marcy:** Right on the next page.

**Max:** So turn it already!

# Chagim

Marcy is right. There are so many holidays that there's practically one for every month of the Jewish year. Some, like Pesach or Chanukah, are well known, but others, like Asarah B'Tevet or Tu B'Av, a lot of people have never heard of. Still, each holiday has its own special message for Jews everywhere. Besides, they can be a lot of fun to celebrate.

# Minhagim

One reason the holidays are so much fun is because they each have their own *minhagim* (customs) and traditions; every holiday is different, and there's always something new to do. Some minhagim go back thousands of years and are written down in the Torah. Others are very new minhagim that are just starting out. Every country and every family has its own minhagim, and you can even make up your own minhagim for your favorite holidays. Who knows? Maybe in a hundred years, everyone will be doing some of the minhagim that you started.

# ימים נוראים

בְּרֹאשׁ הַשָּׁנָה יִכָּתֵבוּן וּבְיוֹם צוֹם כִּפּוּר יֵחָתֵמוּן...

ונתנה תוקף

# YAMIM NORA'IM

On Rosh HaShanah it is written and on Yom Kippur it is sealed...

*U'Netaneh Tokef*

# WHAT ARE ..... THE YAMIM NORA'IM

How would you like to start out the new year? With a big party, like many people do, or by thinking about all the things you did over the past year? What would you like to do again? Is there anything you feel sorry about and think that you can improve?

That's what the Yamim Nora'im are all about. They are ten very serious days (Yamim Nora'im means the "Days of Awe") beginning with Rosh HaShanah, the Jewish New Year, and ending with the fast of Yom Kippur. On these ten days we have a chance to look back at everything we did over the last year and decide what we can try to do better in the coming year. Even if we made some mistakes in the past year - and everybody makes mistakes - the ten days of the Yamim Nora'im are the time to try and make up for it.

## HISTORY

In Jewish tradition, the history of the Yamim Nora'im goes all the way back to the beginning of the world. Some sages say that God created the world on 1 Tishrei, the first day of Rosh HaShanah, which is why it's such an important day.

## THE LAND

Yom Kippur, the last day of the Yamim Nora'im, is a very unusual day in Israel. It's the only day of the year when everything stops. There is no television or radio, no work, no school, no buses, no restaurants, and there are very few cars on the street.

## CUSTOMS

Probably the most important custom on the Yamim Nora'im is the one that so many people like least - apologizing to everyone we may have hurt over the past year. It's an opportunity to visit our friends and say we're sorry for anything bad we may have done to them. Sometimes this can be easy, but most of the time, it's very difficult. It's difficult to admit to someone that you took something from them, or acted rudely, or gossiped about them. And sometimes, when you hurt someone, it's hard to fix afterward. That's what happened to the man who gossiped about the rabbi, when he came to apologize:

"Rabbi," he said, "I'm so sorry. I've been telling all sorts of stories about you, and now I want to apologize. I'll do anything you ask if only you will forgive me."

The rabbi looked at him and said: "You have a feather pillow, don't you? Take it to the middle of the city, wait for the wind to blow, and let all the feathers out. Then collect all the feathers and bring them back to me."

"But Rabbi," the man said, "that's impossible. How can I possibly collect all the feathers. They'll fly everywhere."

The rabbi smiled at him and said: "It's the same with gossip. It goes everywhere and it's so hard to clean up."

Still, we should all try to mend our mistakes, no matter how difficult it seems. And remember, if you want people to forgive you, you should also be ready to forgive them.

**Max:** Marcy, guess what! The teacher invited my whole family to Rosh HaShanah dinner last night.

**Marcy:** She always invites new students and their families for the holidays. How was it?

**Max:** Very strange. I learned a lot, but we ate so many appetizers that I fell asleep before the meal even started.

**Marcy:** You did? That's terrible.

**Max:** What could I do? First we had kiddush, so I had some wine. Then, we had challah with honey. Then we had apples with honey, and then we had pomegranates – I didn't even know what they were. Then we had all these other foods, and then, get this, we had a fish head. Yuck!

**Marcy:** And then what happened?

**Max:** By then I was so stuffed that I fell asleep right at the table.

# Kiddush

Before every meal on Shabbat and holidays, we say kiddush, a prayer ushering in the holiday. We usually say kiddush over wine, to show that this is a festive holiday meal.

# Challah with Honey

Generally we eat salt with the challah bread on Shabbat and holidays. On Rosh HaShanah though, we eat challah with honey to show that we want a sweet year.

# Fish Head

Many people eat the head of a fish on the night of Rosh HaShanah. Before they eat it they say: "May we be as a head and not as a tail."

# Apples with Honey

Before we begin the Rosh HaShanah meal, we eat many special foods that remind us of our prayers for the new year. One of the best known is an apple dipped in honey. Before we eat the apple we say: "May we have a good and sweet year."

# Pomegranates

A pomegranate has many little seeds, which represent the many *mitzvot* (good deeds) we hope to perform during the year. Before we eat the pomegranate we say: "May we have as many good deeds as there are seeds in a pomegranate."

**Max:** Marcy, look what I got! A <u>shofar</u>.

**Marcy:** It's beatiful, Max. Where did you get it?

**Max:** It belonged to my grandfather. My parents let me practice with it for Rosh HaShanah.

**Marcy:** Do you know why we use a shofar?

**Max:** Sure. It's a ram's horn, to remind us of something or other.

**Marcy:** You mean you don't know about the <u>akeidah</u>?

**Max:** Sure I do, with Avraham and Yitzchak and the ram. Say, do you want to hear me play?

**Marcy:** Do you know the notes?

**Max:** Of course: do, re, mi, fa, sol, la, ti.

**Marcy:** No, I mean <u>tekiah, shevarim, teru'ah</u>.

**Max:** Oh, yeah. I've heard of them, but I don't know how to play them.

**Marcy:** You have to practice - it's hard.

## Shofar

The shofar is the ram's horn that we blow on Rosh HaShanah. The sound of the shofar is supposed to wake us up and cause us to do *teshuvah* (repentance).

## Tekiah, Shevarim, Teru'ah

Some people feel so bad about the mistakes they made during the year that they even start to cry. For most people, though, just listening to the notes of the shofar is enough to remind them of crying. The first note, tekiah, sounds like a long wail, shevarim is like three shorter cries, and teru'ah sounds like nine short sobs.

## Akeidah

Another reason we blow the shofar is to remind us of the story of the akeidah. The Torah tells us that God tested Avraham by ordering him to offer his son Yitzchak as a sacrifice. Although Avraham was very upset by this, he did exactly what God told him. He took Yitzchak to a lonely mountain and bound him on an altar (*akeidah* means "binding" in Hebrew). Just as he took out his knife, an angel appeared and told him not to harm his son. God never intended him to sacrifice Yitzchak and only wanted to see if Avraham would obey. Not far from the altar, Avraham noticed a ram tangled in a thorn bush. He removed Yitzchak from the altar and offered the ram instead. Today, we read about the akeidah every Rosh HaShanah to remind us how Avraham was willing to do whatever God told him. We also blow the shofar, to remind us of the ram that Avraham offered instead of his son.

**Max:** Look what I got for a present, Marcy – a new siddur, just for Rosh HaShanah.

**Marcy:** It's not a siddur. It's a <u>machzor</u>.

**Max:** Aha, that's what it is. So how is it different from a siddur?

**Marcy:** It has special prayers for Rosh HaShanah. We say them to show how sorry we are for all the mistakes we made last year.

**Max:** But what if I didn't make any mistakes?

**Marcy:** Everyone makes mistakes, sometimes without noticing.

**Max:** Like on the test we had last week. I made four mistakes.

**Marcy:** No, more like when you hurt someone's feelings or show off. Sometimes you don't notice what you're doing.

**Max:** So what can I do? It's not my fault!

**Marcy:** There's a prayer that tells us exactly what to do. It's called U'Netaneh Tokef and it tells us about three ways to fix our mistakes: <u>teshuvah</u>, or saying we're sorry, <u>tefillah</u>, or praying, and <u>tzedakah</u>, or giving charity.

**Max:** Great. I'm going to start right now... I'm sorry, Marcy.

**Marcy:** And I'm sorry, Max.

## Machzor

For centuries Jews have added prayers and poems of their own to the Yamim Nora'im services. The most popular can be found in the machzor, the special book of prayers we use on these holidays.

## Tefillah

There are many ways to pray. Some people share their feelings with God, others ask Him for help, while still others examine everything they've done and think of ways to act better. Some people pray quietly by themselves. Others come together in a group, or *minyan* (ten Jews). No matter how you pray, though - and most people pray in all these ways at one time or another - the siddur, or prayer book, has prayers for every occasion.

## Teshuvah

The first thing people must do to correct their mistakes is to feel sorry about them and try not to repeat them. In Hebrew this is called teshuvah, which really means "returning." By doing teshuvah, we are returning things to the way they should be.

## Tzedakah

One practical thing anyone can do is giving tzedakah to people who need it. Every day you can put a few coins in a tzedakah box. Then, when the box is full, you can send the money to poor people who need it or to groups that help these people. Another kind of tzedakah you can do without money is gemilut chasadim. All you have to do is help people. Helping a younger brother or sister with their homework, visiting a sick friend, or helping a neighbor carry their groceries home are all ways of doing gemilut chasadim. Can you think of any other ways?

# Rabbi Amnon's Prayer

Everyone knew that Rabbi Amnon was a wise and kind man. Even the duke enjoyed talking with him. "Amnon," he would say, "it's a pity that you're a Jew and cannot go to Heaven."

"You know, my lord," Rabbi Amnon would answer, "Jews believe that God rewards all good people."

The answer only angered the duke. "Amnon," he finally exploded, "convert now or die!"

"Give me three days to decide," Rabbi Amnon begged. The duke agreed, thinking that he would finally listen. After three days, though, Rabbi Amnon did not return. Finally soldiers were sent to arrest him.

"Why didn't you bring me your answer?" the duke raged.

"I was wrong," Rabbi Amnon sighed, "I should have said: 'Sh'ma Yisrael, Adonai Eloheinu Adonai Echad' (Hear O Israel, the Lord is our God, the Lord is One). For that, I must be punished..."

"And punish you I shall," cried the duke.

After hours of torture at the hands of the duke's soldiers, Rabbi Amnon was brought to the synagogue, crippled and dying. It was Rosh HaShanah, and the congregation was about to recite the Kedushah. "Please," he gasped, "open the ark so that I can say one last prayer." The people gathered around to listen. "U'Netaneh Tokef..." Rabbi Amnon finished his prayer and died, but his prayer has become part of the Rosh HaShanah and Yom Kippur service ever since.

# Rabbi Amnon's Prayer - U'Netaneh Tokef

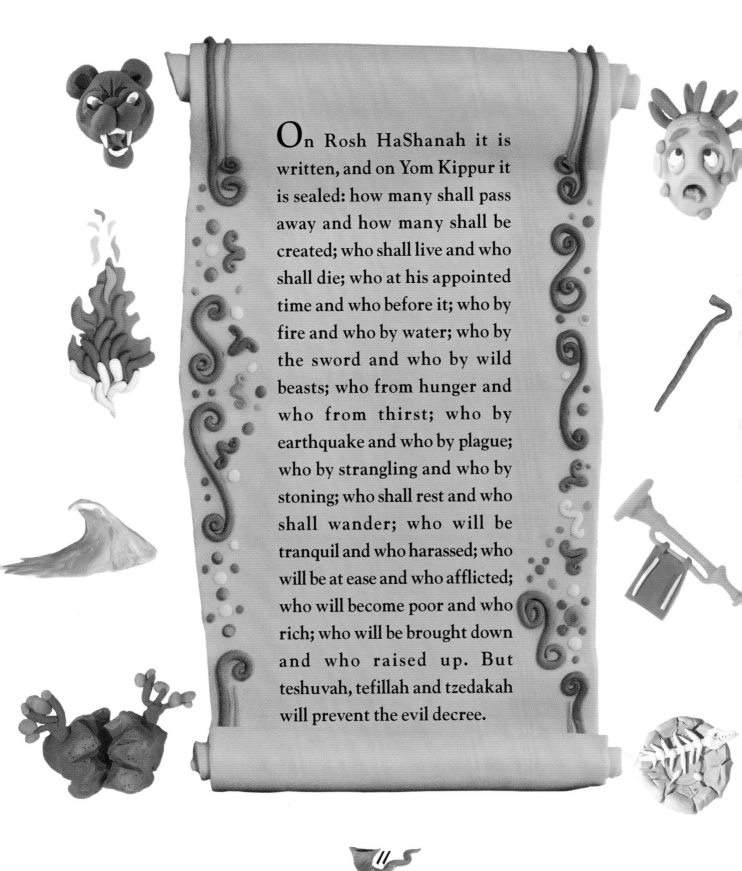

On Rosh HaShanah it is written, and on Yom Kippur it is sealed: how many shall pass away and how many shall be created; who shall live and who shall die; who at his appointed time and who before it; who by fire and who by water; who by the sword and who by wild beasts; who from hunger and who from thirst; who by earthquake and who by plague; who by strangling and who by stoning; who shall rest and who shall wander; who will be tranquil and who harassed; who will be at ease and who afflicted; who will become poor and who rich; who will be brought down and who raised up. But teshuvah, tefillah and tzedakah will prevent the evil decree.

**Marcy:** Max, why did you bring all that bread to the river?

**Max:** It's for <u>tashlich</u>. I'm going to throw it in.

**Marcy:** Crumbs! You're supposed to throw <u>bread crumbs</u>, not four whole loaves of bread!

**Max:** Look, we throw away bread crumbs because they're like our mistakes, right? I don't know about you, but I sure have more mistakes than just a handful of breadcrumbs.

**Marcy:** You'll need a whole bakery just for not listening in school. Don't lean over like that!

**Max:** I want to make sure they get in the water... Whoops!... Hey, the fish are nibbling at me.

**Marcy:** I told you not to lean over like that. Help! Help! Man overboard!

**Max:** Don't worry Marcy. I know how to swim.

## Tashlich

Many Jews have the custom of going to a river or lake or even a well on the first day of Rosh HaShanah. There, they say special prayers declaring that they cast off (*tashlich* in Hebrew) all their sins into the river.

## Bread Crumbs

Once people would empty the lint from their pockets during tashlich to represent the sins that they were casting away. Today, many people have the custom of throwing bread crumbs into the river to represent their sins.

**Marcy:** Max, where are you going with that net?

**Max:** I'm hunting for pigeons. I need them for that thing we do. what did the teacher call it?

**Marcy:** Kapparot?

**Max:** Right. Since the only chickens I found were frozen. I decided to use pigeons instead.

**Marcy:** You know that there's an easier way. Today most people use money for kapparot. Then they give the money to tzedakah.

**Max:** But we can give the chickens to poor people so that they can have a se'udah before the fast.

**Marcy:** We can also give them tzedakah. so that they can buy a meal. Besides. who's going to eat a pigeon. Hey. careful with that net!

**Max:** Look Marcy. here's one. Here birdie! Whoops. sorry Marcy! I guess I should use money for kapparot after all.

## Se'udah

Some rabbis say that it is just as important to eat on the day before Yom Kippur as it is to fast on Yom Kippur itself. That's why, just before the fast begins, we have a big holiday meal, called the *se'udah hamafseket*, the final meal. Then, as soon as the meal is finished, we change into shoes which are not made of leather and go to Beit Knesset for Kol Nidrei.

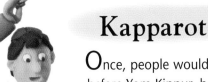

## Kapparot

Once, people would take a chicken before Yom Kippur, hold it over their heads, and ask that the chicken be a substitute for them and receive all the punishments that they deserve. Then they would cook the chicken and feed it to poor people, who didn't have enough food for their se'udah hamafseket. This was called *kapparot*, or atonement. People still do kapparot today, though they generally use money instead of a chicken, then give the money to poor people to buy food.

# A Tale of Two Brothers

A long time ago, on a lonely mountain, lived an old man and his two sons. Even though the boys were forever arguing, they loved their father very much and would never do anything to hurt him. When their father died, they decided to divide their property down the middle.

The older son was already married and had many children who helped him in the fields. He soon became very wealthy. His brother never married and had a hard time making a living as a farmer. Without his father and brother to help him, he became poor, though he always had enough to eat.

One night, the older brother couldn't sleep. "My brother and I always argue, but he is my brother, and my father would have wanted me to help him. I hear that he's become poor. I have more than enough grain here to feed my family. Why don't I take some over to my brother. I'll do it when nobody is watching. That way, he'll never know where it came from."

That same night, the younger brother also couldn't fall asleep. "My brother and I never got along, but he is my brother and my father would have wanted me to help him. With such a big family, he can't possibly have enough food. I don't have very much, but I do have more than I need. Why don't I take some over to him, when no one is watching. That way, he'll never know where the grain came from."

When they woke up the next morning, they were surprised to find that they had the same amount of grain as they did the day before. They both decided to bring more grain to each other the next night, and the next night, and the next night. No matter how much grain they would bring each other, the next day they always had exactly the same amount as before.

One night, as both brothers were coming to the fence, they saw each other carrying a bag of grain. They immediately understood what had been happening every night. Without saying anything, they each dropped their grain and ran to the fence. They hugged each other and apologized for all their years of fighting.

People say that when God saw what happened, He decided that one day He would build His home, the Temple, in that very place. And there God would forgive people's sins, just as the brothers forgave each other.

**Max:** I'm so hungry! I don't know how I'm going to survive this fast.

**Marcy:** But Max, the fast began twenty minutes ago! Besides, you're not even bar mitzvah age yet, so you don't have to fast.

**Max:** I know. I was just thinking about my father. He said he was going to try to fast this year. Tell me Marcy, why do we fast anyway?

**Marcy:** I guess we're supposed to suffer a little after all the mistakes we made. But do you know what else my teacher said last year? One reason we fast is to be like the angels, who don't have to eat or drink or do anything like that.

**Max:** What if I don't fast? Does that mean I'm not like an angel?

**Marcy:** No. There are plenty of other things you can do to be like an angel on Yom Kippur.

**Max:** Like fly around and bless people?

**Marcy:** I was thinking more of not taking a bath or not brushing your teeth.

**Max:** Hurray! I'm almost an angel. I forget to do those things almost every day.

# Fast

On Yom Kippur, Jews try to rise above the physical world. We try to become like angels, who don't need to eat or drink or take care of their bodies. Of course, sick people and children under the age of bar or bat mitzvah are not required to fast on Yom Kippur because it can be dangerous. The most important commandment we have in the Torah is to take care of ourselves and to stay alive, even if it means we have to give up other commandments to do this. In fact, the students of a great rabbi once noticed that he always told sick people to eat on Yom Kippur. "How can you be so careless about the laws of Yom Kippur?" they asked him. "I'm not careless about Yom Kippur, he answered, "I'm just especially careful about *pikuach nefesh* (saving people's lives)."

## Taking a Bath

On Yom Kippur, one way we show that our bodies are not important to us is by not showering or taking baths. We only wash our finger-tips and eyes, and we don't use perfume or deodorant to show that our appearance is less important to us than our actions.

# The Flute

Meir was a good boy. He always listened to his parents and helped out around the house, but no matter how hard he tried, he couldn't learn to read. Instead of going to school, Meir tended his father's cows. Every morning he led them to a meadow, where he would take out his flute and play them the most beautiful tunes. When he put his flute away, the cows knew it was time to go home.

Meir was thirteen when his father took him to the Ba'al Shem Tov on Yom Kippur. "Maybe the presence of such a great man will do Meir some good," his father thought. For a while, it even seemed to work. Meir was excited to be in the same synagogue as the Ba'al Shem Tov, but he was also very sad that he didn't know how to pray.

As the long service came to an end, Meir had an idea. Reaching into his pocket, he pulled out his flute and began to play. "This is how even I can pray," he thought proudly. No one agreed, though; in fact, the entire congregation was outraged. How dare this boy disturb their prayers?

They jumped up from their seats to throw Meir and his father out of the synagogue. Even the Ba'al Shem Tov rushed toward them.

The Ba'al Shem Tov looked at Meir and hugged him. "Thank you," he said. "All Yom Kippur I wondered whether our prayers would be answered. We said all the words, but we lacked the passion. Then I heard your flute, so simple and sincere, and I knew that God was listening." The Ba'al Shem Tov turned to the congregation. "I see you've risen to thank this boy. After all, his flute opened the Gates of Heaven to our prayers."

The Ba'al Shem Tov, a rabbi and teacher who lived in the Ukraine about 250 years ago, taught his students that they can reach God through songs, stories, dances, and sincere prayer just as they could through study. He attracted thousands of followers, who were called *Chasidim*, the "pious ones."

**Marcy:** Are you fidgeting again?

**Max:** I'm sorry. It's just that I've been sitting in this synagogue all day and my foot fell asleep.

**Marcy:** But the prayers are so beautiful. Didn't you like Kol Nidrei last night?

**Max:** Yeah, but I like the Vidui even better, especially when we hit ourselves on the chest. But now I'm waiting till they blow the shofar.

**Marcy:** That's Rosh HaShanah, not Yom Kippur!

**Max:** This time you're wrong! We blow the shofar right after Ne'ilah, before we sing L'Shanah HaBa'ah BiYerushalayim.

**Marcy:** Are you sure?

**Max:** I guess you'll have to wait and see.

# Kol Nidrei

Everyone makes promises, even if they're too hard to keep. Sometimes we also forget about them. But promises are important, especially the ones we make during the Yamim Nora'im to try and improve ourselves. That's why the first prayer that we say just before Yom Kippur begins is Kol Nidrei. Dressed in white, the cantor takes the Torah scrolls out of the ark and parades with them around the synagogue. Then he sings a prayer, saying that all the promises we made during the year, especially the ones we could not keep, should be canceled.

# L'Shanah HaBa'ah BiYerushalayim

The last prayer we say on Yom Kippur is L'Shanah HaBa'ah BiYerushalayim, Next Year in Jerusalem. With Yom Kippur now over, we are excited about all the new year's potential and pray that this will be the year when all Jews will be able to return to Jerusalem and live as a free people in their own land.

# Vidui

One of the best-known prayers during Yom Kippur is the Vidui, or Confession, which we repeat during every service. Before we can feel sorry about our mistakes, we have to admit to ourselves that we actually made them, whether we know it or not. Many centuries ago, the rabbis made a list of all sorts of mistakes, arranged by the letters of the alphabet. Practically every mistake we could possibly make - and a few that we probably couldn't - appears on this list, which everyone recites together, beating their chests each time they name a mistake.

# Ne'ilah

The last part of the service on Yom Kippur is Ne'ilah, or the Closing Service. Tradition tells us that God has already decided what is going to happen to everyone in the coming year. He wrote it all down in a big book and is now putting His seal to it, to show that His decisions are final. Since this is our last chance to show God how sorry we really are, we open the aron (ark) and recite the Ne'ilah service, asking God to take one last look at us and see how we have become better people.

# סוכות

חַג
הַסֻּכּוֹת
תַּעֲשֶׂה לְךָ
שִׁבְעַת
יָמִים
בְּאָסְפְּךָ
מִגָּרְנְךָ
וּמִיִּקְבֶךָ

דברים ט"ז י"ג

---

# SUKKOT

You shall celebrate Sukkot for seven days as you
gather in your crops and the fruit of your vineyards.

*D'varim 16:13*

# WHAT IS.....SUKKOT

In autumn people start spending time indoors. It's a little too cold to be out without a sweater, and in some places it's even starting to snow. But in the middle of autumn we have a holiday, Sukkot, when we are supposed to stay outside - well, actually in a little hut, called a sukkah. For a whole week, life revolves around the sukkah. We eat in it, entertain in it, and in some places, if it's warm enough, even sleep in the sukkah.

The first two days of Sukkot (in Israel it's only one day) are like Shabbat. Instead of going to work or school, many people stay home with their families, go to synagogue... and, of course, spend time in the sukkah. Then come five days of Chol HaMo'ed, which are pretty much like regular days when it comes to work or school, but we still try to spend time in the sukkah, at least when we eat and relax. The last day of Chol HaMo'ed is called Hoshana Rabbah.

As soon as Sukkot is over, we have another short holiday, which lasts two days outside Israel. The first day is called Shmini Atzeret, which means the Gathering of the Eighth Day; the second day is called Simchat Torah, which means Rejoicing with the Torah. When there was a Temple, the Jews held services during Sukkot for the welfare of all the people in the world. According to an ancient legend, as soon as Sukkot was over, God said to the Jewish People: "Now it's time we had a special holiday just for Me and you." On Shmini Atzeret, we pray for a rainy winter so that the farmers in Israel will be able to raise their crops. On Simchat Torah, we celebrate with the Torah. Every Shabbat for an entire year we read the *parashah*, a few chapters from the Torah. On Simchat Torah we read both the last and the first chapters of the Torah, to show that even if we finished reading the Torah, we can start all over again.

## HISTORY

 For forty years the Jews wandered in the desert on their way from Egypt to the Promised Land. They were always on the move, without any time to build a real house. Instead they put up shacks wherever they spent the night. Everyone lived in these huts, from Moshe, the leader, to the poorest people. A long time has passed since then, but once a year we remember what it was like when we left Egypt.

## THE LAND

 Sukkot can be a very happy time for farmers. If they had a good year, they have finished gathering all their crops and they can now relax during the long winter. That's why Sukkot is sometimes called *Chag Ha'Asif*, the Harvest Festival. To show how thankful they were for their crops, people would bring some to the Temple in Jerusalem and offer them to God. While they were there, they would also pray for rain. Since there are no big rivers in Israel, rain is the farmers' main source of water. Even today, on Shmini Atzeret, we still say special prayers for rain.

## CUSTOMS

 There's so much to do on Sukkot. First we build a sukkah, then we decorate it. Once it's ready, we can move into it. On Sukkot we also take the *arba minim*, or four species of plants: a *lulav* (palm branch) and *etrog* (citron - sort of like a lemon), and twigs from a *hadas* (myrtle bush) and an *aravah* (willow). Every morning during Sukkot (except on Shabbat) we carry the arba minim in a parade around the synagogue.

**Marcy:** Max! Where are you going with all those branches?

**Max:** Hi, Marcy! These aren't just branches. These are for s'chach. Don't you remember what the teacher said? Tomorrow is Sukkot, and I'm helping build the sukkah.

**Marcy:** Is there anything I can do?

**Max:** Sure. You can sort out the arba minim while we set up the tables and chairs. Then we'll make decorations.

**Marcy:** Why do we need so many chairs?

**Max:** They're for all the guests.

**Marcy:** Guests? Like who?

**Max:** Well, all the parents and some special guests they call the ushpizin.

**Marcy:** Do you know who they are? Ooh, look at all the beautiful etrogim. They smell so nice.

**Max:** They came all the way from Israel, probably on the same plane as the ushpizin.

**Marcy:** I'm going to have to tell you a little bit about the ushpizin, but before that let's get to work. We have lots to do.

# Arba Minim

A popular explanation for the arba minim (lulav, etrog, hadas and aravah) is that they represent different types of Jews. The etrog tastes and smells good, like Jews who know the Torah and do good deeds. The dates from the lulav taste delicious, but the lulav has no smell, like Jews who know the Torah but don't do good deeds. Hadasim smell good but have no fruit, like those who do good deeds but don't know the Torah. Finally, the aravah has no taste or smell, like those who don't know the Torah and don't do good deeds. We hold the arba minim close together so that the good parts of one make up for what's missing in the others. Only when they are together are they complete.

# Sukkah

The sukkah can have two and a half, three, or four walls (just like the Hebrew letters of the word sukkah). It can be built in a garden, on a balcony, or even on a roof.

# S'chach

These are the branches and twigs we put on top of the sukkah. The s'chach is not a real roof. We can look through it and see the stars at night, reminding us that even inside the sukkah, we are still really outside, with only God protecting us from above.

# Decorations

We try to make the sukkah as beautiful as possible. We can hang fruits and paper chains from the ceiling and pictures on the walls.

# Ushpizin

You can find out who they are at the bottom of each page.

*Chag Sameach! I'm Avraham, the first Jew, and your first guest for Sukkot. My tent was always open to guests, just like your Sukkah is.*

# The Guest

Rabbi Levi Yitzchak of Berdichev had the biggest sukkah in the city. It had to be big. After all, it had to have room for his family, all his students, and plenty of other guests besides. You see, every year on the first night of Sukkot, Rabbi Levi Yitzchak would invite all the strangers in the synagogue to come to his sukkah for dinner. Most of the visitors were very excited by this. After all, it was an honor to be invited to the sukkah of such a great rabbi as Rabbi Levi Yitzchak of Berdichev.

But one year there was a stranger in the town, who turned out to be a very rude guest. While everyone sat quietly around the table, waiting for the rabbi to make kiddush, the stranger poured himself some wine and started picking at the salads. And when people suggested that he should wait, all he said was, "What's taking so long." Pretty soon, everyone was annoyed - everyone, that is except the rabbi. Finally, the rabbi's wife decided to ask her husband how he tolerated such a guest.

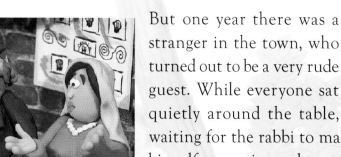

Rabbi Levi Yitzchak smiled at her and said: "In just a few minutes we will be welcoming Avraham Avinu (Avraham our forefather) to our sukkah as our ushpizin guest. I wonder how such a great man can bear to be with people like us. But he does, and every year he comes back again. If he can put up with people like us, I'm sure we can make this special guest feel welcome." And everybody did just that.

Chag Sameach from me, Yitzchak.
I am Avraham's son and I'm the
second ushpizin guest.

22

**Max:** Marcy, are you awake?

**Marcy:** I am now.

**Max:** Sorry. I just can't fall asleep. I never tried sleeping in a sukkah before.

**Marcy:** I know what you mean, but you'd better try and get some sleep. Tomorrow is Chol HaMo'ed and we have school. You know that next year, when I'm in Israel, I won't have school. There the schools are closed for all of Chol HaMo'ed.

**Max:** Wow!

**Marcy:** Not only that, but they even have an extra day of Chol HaMo'ed. Here the second day of the holiday is Yom Tov Sheni Shel Galuyot.

**Max:** So they have even more Chol HaMo'ed than us. I wish I was in Israel for Sukkot. Are the airports closed for Chol HaMo'ed too?

**Marcy:** I don't think so, but anyway, you haven't got a ticket.

**Max:** Hmm, you're right. I can dream about going though.

**Marcy:** Good idea. Now get to sleep.

## Sleeping in a Sukkah

Once the most important mitzvah of Sukkot was sleeping in the sukkah. When the Jews were in exile, they often settled in countries where it was too cold and rainy to continue doing that, so instead, they just ate in the sukkah. In warm places though, especially in Israel, there are still many people who sleep in the sukkah every night of Sukkot.

## Chol HaMo'ed

The last five days of Sukkot are called *Chol HaMo'ed*, the "weekdays of the holiday." We continue living in the sukkah and using the lulav and etrog, but we can also go to work and school and do everything we normally do during the week.

## Yom Tov Sheni Shel Galuyot

Many of the holidays, including Sukkot, are one day shorter in Israel than they are anywhere else. In ancient times, the courts in Jerusalem would announce when the Hebrew month of Tishrei started, and everyone would count fifteen days until Sukkot. But sometimes, it took a long time for the court's decision to reach faraway places, and people celebrated Sukkot on the wrong day. So, it was decided that certain holidays, like Sukkot, would be celebrated for an extra day everywhere except Israel, where people would know the court's decision right away. Even though we now have calendars, we still celebrate *Yom Tov Sheni Shel Galuyot*, the "Second Holiday of the Diaspora," everywhere except Israel.

Chag Sameach! Do you remember me? I'm your guest Ya'akov. I spent a long time being a guest of my father-in-law Laban and of Pharaoh in Egypt.

**Marcy:** Max, hurry up! I don't want to be late for the Simchat Beit HaSho'evah party.

**Max:** Sorry Marcy. I have to get changed first. I thought of doing something special for it and decided to try juggling eggs.

**Marcy:** What happened?

**Max:** Just look at me! Why don't you practice your violin or, better yet, your dancing, while I get dressed?

**Marcy:** Okay. By the way, it's a good thing you didn't try to juggle flaming torches.

**Max:** I wanted to, but my mother got upset.

## Simchat Beit HaSho'evah

# Juggling

This was the name of the party held in the Temple during Chol HaMo'ed Sukkot. It means, "Rejoicing of the House of the Water Drawing," to remind us that only on Sukkot was water poured on the altar as a prayer for rain in the coming winter. Today many people have special parties with music and dancing on the nights of Chol HaMo'ed Sukkot to remember the Simchat Beit HaSho'evah celebration in the Temple.

In the Temple, even the greatest rabbis and teachers would do all sorts of tricks and stunts to show how happy they were during the Simchat Beit HaSho'evah celebration. One highlight was watching Rabban Shimon Ben Gamliel, the wisest man of his time, juggling flaming torches for everyone.

Chag Sameach from me, Moshe. I led the Jews out of Egypt, so I guess you can say I had the first sukkah.

**Max:** Where were you yesterday?

**Marcy:** I went to the country to collect <u>aravot</u> for <u>Hoshana Rabbah</u>.

**Max:** I'm a little confused about Hoshana Rabbah. It's Sukkot, but it's also a little like Yom Kippur.

**Marcy:** That's right. Even though God already decided what's going to happen to us in the coming year, we still have one last chance before He shuts the <u>Gates of Heaven</u>. Today's the last day, so to speak.

**Max:** We still say Hoshanot in the synagogue, don't we?

**Marcy:** Yes, but instead of making just one <u>hakafah</u>, we make seven, and then we take our aravot and beat them against the ground.

**Max:** Now I remember. I think I'll try to behave a lot better next year. Then I won't have to beat my aravot so hard.

## Hakafah

A hakafah is a special parade that we make around the synagogue with our arba minim during Sukkot. Normally we march around the synagogue only once, but on Hoshana Rabbah we go around seven times, each time repeating a different prayer.

## Hoshana Rabbah

The last day of Sukkot is called *Hoshana Rabbah*, or the Great Hoshana. Every day of Sukkot we say special Hoshanot prayers (Hoshana means "Save Us") during the hakafot. On Hoshana Rabbah we repeat all the Hoshanot that we said during Sukkot and add one more, to make seven. We ask God to help us, and if we don't deserve it, we ask Him to help us for the sake of our ancestors, who did deserve it.

## Gates of Heaven

According to Jewish tradition, on Rosh HaShanah God opens the Gates of Heaven to our prayers, decides what will happen to us in the coming year, and writes His decisions in a big book. On Yom Kippur He signs and seals the book. But we still have one last chance - Hoshana Rabbah - to show God that we really mean to be better. Then He closes the Gates of Heaven (though we can still get our prayers in any time if we really try).

## Aravot

When we finish the hakafot, we take five aravot and beat them until the leaves fall off. We hope that our sins fall off us just like the leaves fall off the aravah.

Chag Sameach! It's me.. Aharon the High Priest. When we Jews left Egypt, even God had to live in a temporary house, the Mishkan, where I worked.

**Max:** <u>Shmini Atzeret</u> really is a strange day! Everybody's praying for rain but it's already raining!

**Marcy:** We're not praying for ourselves. We say <u>Tefillat HaGeshem</u> for the farmers in Israel, who need the rain for their crops. By the way, did you hear the weather forecast?

**Max:** They said it will stop raining tonight.

**Marcy:** That's good, because tomorrow is <u>Simchat Torah</u>, and everyone will be dancing in the streets.

# Simchat Torah

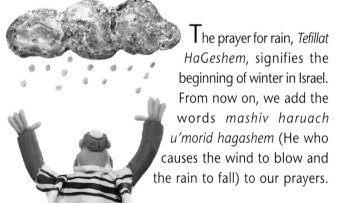

Simchat Torah is the last day of a long holiday season that began with Rosh HaShanah. It is a very happy day, as you will find out on the next page.

# Tefillat HaGeshem

The prayer for rain, *Tefillat HaGeshem*, signifies the beginning of winter in Israel. From now on, we add the words *mashiv haruach u'morid hagashem* (He who causes the wind to blow and the rain to fall) to our prayers.

# Shmini Atzeret

Right after Sukkot comes a new holiday, Shmini Atzeret. We no longer use the sukkah or parade around the synagogue with the arba minim. Now that Sukkot is over, we can pray for rain.

Chag Sameach! I'm Yosef. Too bad the holiday is over. Your sukkah was just as colorful as my coat.

**Marcy:** Here Max, grab a flag and stick an apple on the end.

**Max:** Thanks Marcy. I'm all ready for the hakafot. How do I look?

**Marcy:** Fine, I guess. Why are you so worried?

**Max:** Because I'm having my first aliyah today, with all the other boys, during Kol HaNe'arim.

**Marcy:** Wow! That is exciting! If you keep it up you may be Chatan Torah one day. Did I tell you who Chatan Breishit is?

**Max:** No, but I already heard that it's your father. That's quite an honor. Mazal Tov!

**Marcy:** And Mazal Tov to you on your first aliyah.

## Chatan Torah

On Simchat Torah we read Zot HaBrachah, the last parashah of the Torah. The very last person to have an aliyah is usually one of the most respected members of the congregation, like the rabbi. The person who gets this aliyah is called *Chatan Torah*, the Torah's bridegroom.

## Kol HaNe'arim

Even the children go up to the Torah for an aliyah on Simchat Torah. They stand together under a big tallit and recite the brachot together before and after the Torah is read. When they are done, their parents throw candies at them.

## Aliyah

This word means "going up" in Hebrew. We go up when we move to Israel, and we go up to make the brachot and read from the Torah. Usually, only a few people have an aliyah to the Torah, but on Simchat Torah everyone in the synagogue has an aliyah.

## Chatan Breishit

Right after the Chatan Torah finishes his aliyah, the Torah is rolled back to the beginning and another person is called up for the first aliyah from the Book of Breishit. The person who gets this aliyah is called *Chatan Breishit*, the groom of the Book of Breishit. This aliyah is also reserved for a respected member of the community, like Marcy's father.

## Hakafot

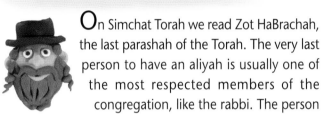

On Sukkot we marched around the synagogue with the arba minim. On Simchat Torah we march around the synagogue seven times carrying the Torah scrolls.

*Chag Sameach from me, King David! Did you know that before I was a king, I was a shepherd. Then I used to live in a sukkah all year round.*

# A Soviet Simchat Torah

"Hey, Lev! Come on. I have a test tomorrow and I have to study."

"Me too, Alex, but just listen to all that noise. I wonder what it is?"

"It sounds like it's coming from the synagogue. Don't you want to check it out?"

"I don't know. Remember what Dad told us about going there."

"But how will he ever find out? Look over there. People are dancing in the street. What's going on?"

"Wait a minute. It must be that holiday that Grandpa told me about. What did he call it ... I know, Simchat Torah or something like that."

"Right, I remember now. That's when everyone goes to the synagogue."

"Everyone except Dad. Let's go!"

Are you sure about this? What will Dad say if he finds out?"

"Well, Alex, he's not going to find out. Besides, practically all the Jews in town will be at the synagogue."

"Why is that?"

"I don't know. But I hear that people take Simchat Torah pretty seriously."

The two boys walked over to the synagogue. They were frightened, but at the same time they were glad to have this opportunity to meet so many Jews. And there were so many, in fact, that they couldn't reach the door. Even the street was packed with

people. The boys knew many of them, but many others were a complete surprise. "Look at that," said Alex, "I didn't know that he was Jewish." It took just a few seconds for the boys to be swept into a big circle of people

Chag Sameach! I'm King Shlomo, who wrote the scroll of Kohelet, which we read on Shabbat Chol HaMo'ed.

dancing a hora. "Hey Alex," Lev called out, "Do you think we could get some flags?" In fact, many of the children were dancing with colorful Simchat Torah flags.

Lev felt a tap on his shoulder. "Did I hear you boys say you want some flags?"

"Thanks, Dad!" he said. "Dad! Oh no! Alex, we're caught!"

"That's right," their father said, "What are you doing here?"

Their smiles disappeared quickly. "But Dad," Lev answered, "we just wanted to see what Simchat Torah was like."

Alex was just as surprised as his father was. "And what are you doing here, Dad?"

Their father just smiled, "I guess we all wanted to see what Simchat Torah was like. I won't tell your mother if you don't." The boys winked at their father and dragged him into the circle of dancers. And in a far corner, a woman beamed happily. After all, she hardly expected to see her husband and sons at the synagogue on Simchat Torah.

 **Max:** You lied to me, Marcy. Don't talk to me!

**Marcy:** I lied? What's the matter?

**Max:** You promised that there would be a holiday every month. Today the teacher said there's no holiday this month. I want a holiday in November too!

**Marcy:** First of all, the teacher didn't say anything about November. She said Marcheshvan.

**Max:** Mar who? Mar Heshenbaum, the new teacher from Israel?

**Marcy:** No, Marcheshvan, that's the name of the Jewish month.

**Max:** Oh, I remember the teacher said something about a Jewish calendar. I didn't understand her though.

**Marcy:** I have an idea. Didn't you get a telescope for your birthday?

**Max:** Yeah, it's great. I can see the moon and all the stars with it.

**Marcy:** Go get it and meet me on the next page. I'll explain the Jewish calendar to you there.

## Marcheshvan

The month of Cheshvan is the only month in the Jewish calendar that has no special days. Some say this is why we call it *Mar-Cheshvan*, or Bitter Cheshvan. According to another legend, all the months got together to cheer up Cheshvan by giving it a title, Mar, or Mister.

## Jewish Calendar

The Jewish holidays are celebrated according to the Jewish calendar. It has twelve months - Tishrei, Cheshvan, Kislev, Tevet, Shvat, Adar, Nisan, Iyar, Sivan, Tammuz, Av, and Elul - though sometimes, on leap years, an extra month, Adar Bet, is added.

**Max:** Here's the telescope. It's so heavy! Why do you need it?

**Marcy:** Let's set it up and you'll see. Tell me if you can see the <u>moon</u>.

**Max:** Hey, there it is. Wow, look how tiny it is! I can hardly see it.

**Marcy:** That's right. This is <u>Rosh Chodesh</u>, or the beginning of the new Jewish month.

**Max:** Rosh Chodesh? Hmm, that's sort of like Rosh HaShanah, right.

**Marcy:** Right. Rosh HaShanah is the start of the New Year, and Rosh Chodesh is the start of the new month. It begins as soon as we see the new moon.

**Max:** What did people do before they had telescopes?

**Marcy:** A long time ago the court in Jerusalem would decide when it was Rosh Chodesh. As soon as witnesses saw the moon they would run and tell the court. Then, the court would proclaim that the new month had begun and light a <u>bonfire</u> on top of a high mountain. Everyone who saw the bonfire knew that it was Rosh Chodesh. By the way, they also threw a big party in honor of the witnesses.

**Max:** Hey, I saw the moon first, so you have to throw me a party.

**Marcy:** How about some milk and cookies.

**Max:** Good enough!

## Rosh Chodesh

Rosh Chodesh is celebrated for one or two days, depending on the length of the month before. If it's 29 days, Rosh Chodesh is celebrated on the first day of the new month; if it's 30 days, it is celebrated on the last day of the old month and the first day of the new month. Rosh Chodesh was once a very important holiday in the Temple. Today we remember Rosh Chodesh by saying special prayers and reading the Torah in the synagogue.

## Bonfire

As soon as people far away saw the bonfire announcing the new month, they would also light fires on mountains near them. In a few hours there would be a chain of bonfires stretching from Jerusalem to Babylonia and everyone would know that it was Rosh Chodesh.

## Moon

The calendar we normally use is based on the time it takes for the Earth to orbit the sun - 365 days. The Jewish calendar is based on how long it takes the moon to orbit the Earth - 29 and a half days. Since twelve months of 29 or 30 days don't equal a whole year, the holidays will change seasons every few years. That's why, in ancient times, the sages decided to add an extra leap month every few years - so Chanukah always comes out in winter and Pesach always comes out in spring.

חֲנוּכָּה

# CHANUKAH

And all the eight days of Chanukah these candles are holy...

*Prayer for Chanukah*

וְכָל
שְׁמוֹנַת
יְמֵי חֲנֻכָּה
הַנֵּרוֹת
הַלָּלוּ
קֹדֶשׁ
הֵם...

תפילה לחנוכה

# What is.....Chanukah

Take a look out your window this evening. It's snowy outside, and dark too, because in winter the days are so short. It's Chanukah, and in Israel and in many places around the world Jews are lighting candles in their windows as night falls. They're adding a little light to the world and reminding everyone of the miracles that happened to their ancestors so long ago.

## History

 Over two thousand years ago, the Jews of Israel were ruled by the Greek conquerors of Syria. At first, the Jews admired the Greeks and many Jews tried to become more like them. They spoke Greek, wore Greek clothing, and sometimes even observed the Greek religion. Of course, there were also many Jews who refused to become like the Greeks. Antiochus, the Greek king, wanted all his subjects to live like Greeks, so he made laws forbidding Jews to practice their religion.

Antiochus wasn't the only ruler to make such laws. At one time or another, the same thing happened almost everywhere Jews lived. Sometimes Jews kept the new laws and sometimes they had to leave the country. In the time of Antiochus, the Jews revolted.

At first there was only a handful of rebels, hiding in the mountains and living like partisans. Soon many people joined them, and in a short time the rebels had a whole army fighting the Greeks. After many long years, the Jews finally threw the Greek army out of the country. The first thing they did as soon as they conquered Jerusalem, was to rededicate the Temple (*Chanukah* means "dedication"). When they tried to light the menorah, all they could find was enough oil to last them for one day. A miracle happened and the little jar of oil burned for eight days.

## The land

 In Israel, practically every building has a *chanukiah* (Chanukah menorah) during Chanukah. You can find chanukiot on top of the *Knesset* (Israel's parliament), at city hall, at the *Kotel* (the Western Wall), and even lining the streets.

## Customs

 Ever since then, Jews have celebrated the victory over the Greeks during the holiday of Chanukah. On the first night we light one candle, on the second night we light two candles, and so on. By the eighth night we have eight candles burning brightly, reminding us of the eight days that the oil burned in the Temple and of the Jewish struggle against oppression.

**Max:** Look Marcy, I think this chanukiah, is defective. I can't get my candles to stay in the little cu

**Marcy:** Those aren't for candles.

**Max:** What? You mean it's electric? So where's the plug?

**Marcy:** Oh Max! It's for olive oil, just like the menorah in the Temple.

**Max:** I knew that! I was just testing you. Now I have to figure out where to light it.

**Marcy:** What about on your window sill? That way everyone can see it.

**Max:** Well, my mother always tells me not to show off.

**Marcy:** It's not showing off. It's called pirsumei nisa, telling everyone about the Chanukah miracle. Everyone who sees the lights burning will remember the story.

**Max:** Or else they can read the story on the next page.

# Pirsumei Nisa

*Pirsumei nisa*, or publicizing the miracle, is a very important custom on Chanukah. We light the candles in a window or by a door facing the street so that everyone passing by will see them and remember the miracles that happened. Today, you can even find the Chanukah story and chanukiot on the Internet.

# Chanukiah

The special menorah we use on Chanukah is called a chanukiah in Hebrew. It has places for eight candles and an extra place for the *shamash* - the candle we use to light all the other candles.

# Candles

Even though electric light bulbs shine brighter than candles, we use candles on Chanukah, to remind us of the burning lamps of the menorah.

# Olive Oil

In ancient times, people used lamps filled with oil instead of candles. Today some people still use oil in their chanukiot instead of candles, just like they did in in the Temple.

# The Uprising

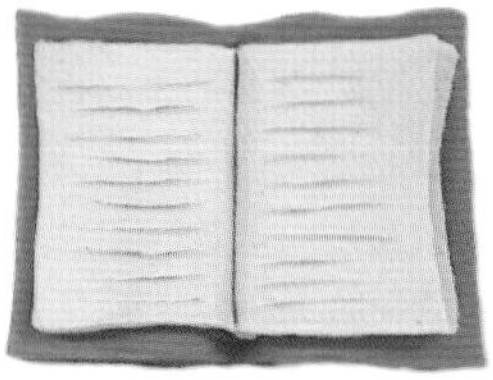

Matityahu was angry. Jews everywhere were beginning to act like Greeks. They had little choice, of course. King Antiochus refused to let them study the Torah or keep the mitzvot. Still, what happened yesterday was too much. Who would have believed that in his own village, Modi'in, Jews would sacrifice to the Greek gods? Would his own sons one day do the same?

That's why he called them home last night. They were all there: Elazar, Shimon, Yochanan, Yonatan and Yehudah. They argued for hours. Matityahu could still hear Yehudah hammering the table with his fist. "We must throw Antiochus and his soldiers out of our country before there are no Jews left." As the sun began to rise, they packed their bags and said goodbye to their families.They had to hurry so that they would get to town on time.

The town square looked like a carnival. There were flags and streamers everywhere, and everyone was dressed in their best clothes. In the middle of the square was an enormous statue. "It's Zeus," people explained, but to Matityahu it looked just like a statue of Antiochus. Today the mayor would say a prayer to the statue. Then he would sacrifice a pig to the Greek god. "I never thought I'd see you here," a neighbor whispered, as Matityahu and his sons pushed to the front of the crowd.

Before them was the mayor, clean-shaven and wearing a Greek tunic. Yonatan

tugged at Matityahu's sleeve: "Look how many soldiers! Maybe we should wait." He already knew his father's answer.

Suddenly Matityahu jumped in front of the mayor and knocked the statue to the ground. Everyone stared, amazed that an old man could have such strength. The soldiers rushed at Matityahu, but his sons pulled out their swords and formed a circle around him. "*Mi laShem, eilai* - Whoever is for God, follow me!" Two neighbors joined them, then a farmer, then a shopkeeper. The soldiers charged, but the crowd closed in, hiding Matityahu and his sons. The revolt had begun.

35

**Marcy:** Did you spend your <u>Chanukah gelt</u> already?

**Max:** Not yet. I haven't decided what I want to do with it.

**Marcy:** Let me help you get rid of some of it. Bring some change to my Chanukah party tonight.

**Max:** Are you going to sell the <u>latkes</u> and <u>sufganiyot</u>?

**Marcy:** No, those are free. We're going to play <u>dreidel.</u>

**Max:** What, we're going to play for money?

**Marcy:** Of course, people have been playing dreidel like that for centuries.

**Max:** Wow, that means I get all of your Chanukah gelt too, if I win.

**Marcy:** What if I win?

**Max:** Not a chance!

**Marcy:** Well, if I do win, I'll buy you a Chanukah present.

## Latkes

Since the miracle of Chanukah happened through a jar of oil, one way to remember the miracle is to eat foods cooked in oil during Chanukah. *Latkes*, or potato pancakes fried to a crispy, golden brown, are one popular Chanukah food.

## Chanukah Gelt

There's an old custom of giving children gifts of coins on Chanukah. Sometimes the coins are real and sometimes they are made of chocolate. Today, many children also get other Chanukah presents when we light the menorah.

## Sufganiyot

Another popular Chanukah treat is *sufganiyot*, or jelly doughnuts, also fried in oil. In Israel sufganiyot are sold everywhere during Chanukah.

## Dreidel

Dreidels are a favorite toy on Chanukah. They are four-sided tops with Hebrew letters painted or carved on the sides. The letters - *nun, gimel, heh*, and *shin* - stand for the Hebrew words: "*Nes gadol hayah sham*" (A great miracle happened there). One way to play dreidel is to spin it for money. Everyone puts a coin in the pot, then they spin the dreidel to see who wins: nun means nothing - you don't have to put in another coin and you don't get anything; gimel means you get everything in the pot; heh means you get half of what is in the pot; and shin means you have to put one into the pot. In Israel a dreidel is called a *sevivon*. The sevivon has a *peh* instead of a *shin* on one side, so that the letters stand for "*Nes gadol hayah poh*" (A great miracle happened here).

# The Miracle of the Oil

Yehudah HaMaccabee slowed down as he reached the heavy gold doors of the Temple. He had seen many miracles over the past few years. His army of Jews won many battles; they threw the Greeks out of Jerusalem. Just yesterday they liberated the Temple, but when they went inside, all they found was a terrible mess. There were idols everywhere, and all the sacred vessels were desecrated. In a corner stood the menorah, tarnished and dusty after so many years. "Find me olive oil," Yehudah ordered, "Let's light the menorah as a sign of our freedom."

All they could find was one small jar, enough for a day, if they were lucky. The other jars had been opened by the Greeks and could no longer be used, but it would take at least a week - eight days, more likely - to make more oil. "Light the menorah," he ordered. "We will do what we have to do, and God will take care of the rest." They poured the oil carefully, so as not to spill a single drop. The seven lamps cast a bright light over the room. Yehudah wanted to stay and watch them burn, but he knew that he would have to leave soon. Antiochus and his soldiers were not yet defeated.

The next morning Yehudah received a strange message. "The menorah is still burning, as if no oil was used up." He ran to see the miracle for himself and then he knew that the menorah would stay lit until new oil was made. He knew that next year Jews would celebrate the miracle of the oil and remember the miracle of a few determined men, who defeated the most powerful army in the world.

**Marcy:** I'm so nervous. This is my first Maccabiah. I've been practicing gymnastics for half a year already.

**Max:** Check out my new judo outfit. When I grow up, I'm going to be in the Maccabiah in Israel and then in the Olympics. I wonder how many Maccabees were in the Olympics in ancient times.

**Marcy:** None of them. They were fighting against Greek culture being forced on them. The Olympics were Greek, so they would have been against them.

**Max:** So why do we call the big Jewish sporting event the Maccabiah? And why are we having our sports competition today, on Chanukah?

**Marcy:** I asked the teacher that yesterday. She explained that it's okay to learn things from other cultures as long as we don't give up our own culture to do it. Other people borrowed ideas from Jewish culture.

**Max:** Like the Ten Commandments.

**Marcy:** Right, and we borrowed the Olympics from the Greeks and made them Jewish.

**Max:** Too bad I can't make Santa Claus Jewish.

## Maccabiah

Every four years, Jewish athletes from around the world gather in Israel for the Maccabiah Games. These games provide a unique opportunity for young Jews to meet, compete in sports and have a good time together. Many famous athletes participate in the games - some of them even go on to win medals in the Olympics - but there are also many people who belong to Jewish sports clubs around the world, who just come to enjoy the Maccabiah and make new friends.

## Ten Commandments

Jews can be very proud of the many aspects of their culture that have been adopted by other people. One of the greatest Jewish contributions to the world has been the Ten Commandments, which are now the basis of the moral code in so many places around the world.

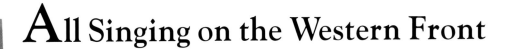

# All Singing on the Western Front

Captain Yakov Lazarov looked sadly at his medals. "Four medals, and here I am on the fourth night of Chanukah, in a trench, face to face with the German Army." In the past week, the quiet meadow where he camped with his troops had become a sea of mud, pockmarked with shell craters. He was homesick, and he even thought he could smell his wife's latkes frying somewhere far away.

Most of his troops were heading to the forest to find a Christmas tree. "If they can celebrate, so can I," he said, arranging his medals on the edge of the trench. He wondered where his family was and if they remembered it was Chanukah. Was his son arranging bottle caps on a window sill at home? "I'm sure he has all four candles, while

all I have is one. Still, it should be enough. Maybe I'll even have a Chanukah miracle." He cut the candle into four and mounted each piece on a medal. Then he waited for the wind to die down. "*Baruch ata...*," he began to sing, quietly at first, but gradually louder, "...*lehadlik ner shel Chanukah*." He thought he heard Amen echoing across the meadow. "The wind really does play tricks on you," he laughed. "*Baruch ata...*" he sang again, "*ba'yamim hahem bazman hazeh*." Again the wind whistled Amen.

"*Ma'oz tzur yeshu'ati*." He didn't know all the words by heart so he began to whistle the rest. "*Lecha na'eh leshabe'ach*," answered the wind. "That's not the wind!" Yakov said as he looked around. It was a private, lying in a trench, not even fifty yards away. "*Tikon beit tefilati...*" This one came from behind him; it was the quarter-master. "*V'sham todah nezabe'ach*," this time it was the private with a bandage over his forehead. Then someone else picked up the tune, then someone else, adding a line, a phrase, a word. The quarter-master inched forward carrying a plate of... could it be... yes... latkes! "A *Freiliche Chanuke*, Captain," he shouted, "Happy Chanukah, everyone."

**Max:** Marcy, can I share your sandwich? I forgot my lunch.

**Marcy:** Sure you can. Do you know some of the adults aren't eating today?

**Max:** Good! I thought some of the teachers needed to go on a diet.

**Marcy:** Don't you know? It's because of <u>Asarah B'Tevet</u>.

**Max:** You mean it's another holiday? Then what are we doing in school? I'm going home.

**Marcy:** Hang on a second. It's not that kind of holiday. It's a <u>fast day</u> to commemorate the destruction of the walls of Jerusalem over twenty-five hundred years ago. This was the beginning of the <u>Galut</u>.

**Max:** But anyone can go to Israel today. You're going next year, aren't you?

**Marcy:** You're right. But there's another reason too. In Israel it was decided that Asarah B'Tevet would be <u>Yom HaKaddish HaKlali</u>, a Day of Memorial for the Jews who died in the <u>Sho'ah</u>.

**Max:** In that case, I guess I'll manage without your sandwich today.

## Fast Day

Throughout the Jewish calendar there are several fast days to commemorate terrible things that happened to the Jewish People in the past. Many of these fast days, including Asarah B'Tevet, recall events that surrounded the destruction of the Temple.

## Galut

Ever since the destruction of the First Temple, most Jews have lived in Exile, or Galut. Some of the countries in which they lived were very good to them; in other countries the Jews were oppressed, but no matter where they lived, they always dreamed of one day going back to their ancient homeland of Israel.

## Sho'ah

The Sho'ah was the murder of six million Jews during the Holocaust by the Nazis and their accomplices. You can find out more about the Sho'ah on page 61.

## Asarah B'Tevet

The tenth day of the Hebrew month of Tevet, commemorates the Babylonian siege of Jerusalem that ended with the destruction of the First Temple. This was the first stage in the conquest of Jerusalem, that led to the exile of the Jews from the Land of Israel.

## Yom HaKaddish HaKlali

No one knows exactly when so many of the millions of Jews who perished in the Sho'ah actually died. Many families were wiped out, and no one was left to say *kaddish*, the prayer for the dead, for them. In Israel the Chief Rabbis decided that on Asarah B'Tevet, kaddish would be said for all those who have no one left to say kaddish for them, and by people who lost families in the Sho'ah, but do not know exactly when their relatives died.

ט"ו בִּשְׁבָט
הִגִּיעַ,
חַג
לָאִילָנוֹת...
שיר עממי

# ט"ו בשבט

## TU BISHVAT

Tu BiShvat has arrived - a holiday for trees...

*Folk song*

**Marcy:** Where are you going all bundled up like that?

**Max:** Don't you know it's Tu BiShvat. I'm going to plant a tree.

**Marcy:** Max, there's a blizzard outside. You can't plant a tree now.

**Max:** Look, the teacher said that on Tu BiShvat we plant trees.

**Marcy:** She meant in Israel, where they don't have three feet of snow on the ground – but you can put some coins in this little blue box to buy trees in Israel. Next year, if you want, I'll plant one there for you.

**Max:** Plant me an apple tree. It's my favorite.

**Marcy:** Anything you want.

**Max:** Good, then plant me an apple tree and send me all my apples.

## Tu BiShvat

Even though it's winter outside, in Israel the trees are starting to blossom. To mark the first signs of spring, we celebrate Tu BiShvat, the New Year of Trees.

## Blue Box

When Jews began coming back to Israel, they planted trees everywhere to restore the ancient landscape. To collect money for this enormous project, little blue boxes were sent to every community in the Diaspora. That way, no matter where Jews lived, they could collect coins to help the settlers in Israel bring the country back to life.

## Plant a Tree

One way to celebrate Tu BiShvat is by planting trees. This is especially important in Israel. A hundred years ago there were very few trees there. Now there are beautiful forests everywhere.

A man once went on a long trip through the desert. He was very thirsty – so thirsty that he wasn't sure he could continue. Suddenly, he saw an enormous tree with shady branches, delicious fruit and, could it be? Yes, a pool of water beside it. The man ran to the tree, drank the water, ate the fruit, and took a nap in the shade. Finally, it was time to leave. "How can I bless you?" he asked the tree. "You are already big and shady, you have such delicious fruit, and there is a pool of sweet water right next to you. "Tree," he continued, "may all the saplings cut from you grow up to be just like you."

# His Friend, the Tree

Ilan sat on the grass crying. This was where his friend had lived, and every day Ilan came to remember him.

They were both born on the same day, Tu BiShvat. As soon as Ilan's father heard that he had a son, he planted an apple tree in the garden. Over the years, Ilan and the tree became the best of friends. He often climbed it, and once he even fell off and had to wear a cast. When he came back from the doctor, he ran straight to the tree to tell it about his adventures. A swing was hanging from one of its branches.

"Until you get better," his father warned him, "I don't want you climbing that tree. You can play on the swing instead."

When Ilan got older, he courted his girlfriend in the shade of the tree. Sometimes he even gave her apples. "These are love apples," he joked, "from my friend the tree to you."

A few months later, when Ilan got married, twigs and leaves from the tree were woven into his *chuppah*.

Years later, on a stormy night, Ilan's son came down with a fever. To keep him warm, Ilan gathered some dry branches from the tree and put them in the fireplace. In a few days, his son was better. On Shabbat, Ilan held a party to celebrate his son's recovery. Everyone ate apple cake, made out of juicy, red apples from his friend, the tree.

Ilan was already old and wrinkled, just like his friend the tree. It was difficult for Ilan to move around, and the tree had very few apples left. One cold autumn night, in the middle of a thunder storm, a bolt of lightning struck Ilan's friend, the tree. There was a loud crash as it toppled to the ground. Ilan ran to the window to see what happened, but all he could see was a strange, empty space, where his friend, the tree, once stood. "Goodbye, my friend," he whispered, as he piled the burnt branches outside his house.

One day, however, Ilan noticed a leaf poking through the grass. The next day there were two and even a tiny stalk. After a few days, Ilan took his grandchildren to visit the sapling. "My friend is gone," he told them, "but his child has come to keep me company. Promise me that you will always take care of him."
And they did.

# פורים

## PURIM

וִימֵי הַפּוּרִים
הָאֵלֶּה לֹא
יַעַבְרוּ מִתּוֹךְ
הַיְּהוּדִים
וְזִכְרָם
לֹא־יָסוּף
מִזַּרְעָם.

אסתר ט' כ"ח

And these days of Purim will never pass from the Jewish people, and the memory will not be forgotten by their descendants.

*Esther 9:28*

# WHAT IS.... PURIM

Why is the teacher dressed like a witch? And the boy in the back, he's dressed like a cowboy. Just look in the mirror. You're dressed like a clown. Something strange is going on here. Purim must be right around the corner. Purim is the happiest day in the Jewish year - the sages used to say that as soon as the month of Adar starts, everyone becomes happier. But Purim is also the oddest day of the year. In fact, on Purim everything goes topsy-turvy. The strong become weak, winners become losers, and everyone becomes someone else as soon as they put on their costumes.

## THE LAND

Purim is one big party, celebrating how the Jews of Persia defeated their enemies who tried to destroy them. In Shushan, the Persian capital, the fighting took an extra day, so the parties started one day later. We remember this by celebrating Purim one day later in Jerusalem, our own capital. When most people are getting over their Purim parties, the people of Jerusalem are just getting ready to start theirs.

## HISTORY

Purim is based on events that took place in Persia 2,500 years ago, after the First Temple was destroyed but before the Second Temple was built. Most Jews lived in exile then, and were subject to the whims of kings like Achashverosh.

## CUSTOMS

Max will find out about many Purim customs, like reading the Megillah or giving mishloach manot. Another custom is to give *matanot l'evyonim*, or gifts to poor people, on Purim. That way, even they can have a happy Purim, with lots of good food and wine.

**Max:** Marcy, why aren't you in class.

**Marcy:** I got kicked out.

**Max:** You! You got kicked out! How?

**Marcy:** The teacher was telling us about the <u>Megillah</u> and every time she said Haman, I picked up my <u>gragger</u> and made noise. Say, why aren't you in class?

**Max:** I got kicked out too.

**Marcy:** What did you do?

**Max:** My mother baked some <u>hamentashen</u> and I ate them in class.

**Marcy:** Do you have any left?

**Max:** No, the teacher took them away and said they'd be my <u>mishloach manot</u> to him.

**Marcy:** We'd better go to my house. My mother is baking hamentashen for the <u>se'udah</u> right now.

## Megillah

The Megillah is a scroll that contains the story of Purim. Often the Megillah is richly decorated with pictures from the Purim story. We read the Megillah twice on Purim, once in the evening and once in the morning.

## Hamentashen

Different Jewish communities have special foods for Purim, which remind them of the story and poke fun at Haman. Ashkenazi Jews often eat *hamentashen*, three-cornered cookies stuffed with jam, chocolate, or poppy seeds. They are supposed to resemble Haman's three-cornered hat. Sephardi Jews often eat *oznei Haman*, long, pointy cookies, which are supposed to resemble Haman's ears.

## Mishloach Manot

Another popular custom on Purim is to bring gifts of food to friends and relatives. This way we can share our happiness with others by giving them cakes, candy, fruits and all sorts of other good things to eat.

## Gragger

It's difficult to forget what Haman tried to do, but we still want to wipe out every reminder of him, even when we tell the story about how we were rescued. That's why, when we read the story of Purim in the Megillah, we make as much noise as possible every time Haman's name is mentioned. Some people write "Haman" on the soles of their shoes and stamp their feet on the ground when they hear his name. Others have a special rattle, called gragger in Yiddish or *ra'ashan* in Hebrew, which they use to make a racket.

## Se'udah

On the day of Purim we have a big meal called the se'udah to celebrate the holiday. At the se'udah many adults drink wine so that they get a little tipsy. The se'udah reminds us of all the parties King Achashverosh threw. He was drunk when he decided to kill the Jews and he was drunk when he decided to save them.

**Marcy:** Max, what's the matter?

**Max:** I can't find Stanley. He's my co-star in the Purim shpiel.

**Marcy:** You're also in the play. Let me guess your part - Achashverosh?

**Max:** Nope.

**Marcy:** Haman?

**Max:** Uh uh!

**Marcy:** I know you're not Mordechai because I'm Esther, and you probably aren't Vashti.

**Max:** Right!

**Marcy:** And why do you need Stanley? Are you two the guards that Mordechai overheard plotting?

**Max:** Much more important than that. Hey, here's Stanley now.

**Marcy:** I get it. You're the horse that Mordechai rode. Stanley's the head and you're...

**Max:** That's right, the most important part of all - the part that Mordechai rides on. Come on Stanley. Let's practice the rest of the play. Neigh!

## Purim Shpiel

Another popular Purim custom is to perform funny plays called Purim shpiels which tell the story of Purim. In some of these plays, performed in Jewish schools and community centers, students sometimes even imitate their teachers and rabbis in ways that won't hurt their feelings.

## Achashverosh

He was king of Persia, a very rich and powerful man. Only, he wasn't happy with his wife, Queen Vashti. One day, when the king was drunk, he had her banished. Now King Achashverosh was a very lonely man.

## Haman

At about the same time, Haman, one of King Achashverosh's advisor's became a very important person in Persia. Achashverosh agreed to do everything Haman told him, and Haman asked for a lot. He even wanted people to bow down to him.

## Mordechai

He refused to bow down to Haman. When Haman found out that Mordechai was Jewish, he decided to get Achashverosh to kill all the Jews. The King agreed.

## Esther

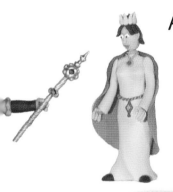

A few months earlier, Achashverosh held a contest to find someone to replace Vashti as queen. The most beautiful girl he found was Esther, Mordechai's niece. At first, she did not tell the king that she was Jewish.

## Guards

One day, Mordechai overheard two guards discussing ways to kill Achashverosh. He told Esther, who told the king, and the two guards were executed.

## Horse

Many months later, Achashverosh decided to reward Mordechai. He asked Haman what to do to a person whom the king wants to honor. Haman thought Achashverosh meant him, and said that the person should be led through the city, wearing the king's robes and riding the king's horse. Achashverosh said: "Do it to Mordechai."

## Rest of the Play

Esther was now ready to tell the king who she was and what Haman wanted to do to her uncle. When Achashverosh heard about it, he had Haman executed. Thanks to Esther and Mordechai, the Jews were saved.

# The Frankfurt Purim

In many communities around the world, Jews were saved from persecution, just as they were on Purim. On the anniversary of the day that they were saved, they made a special holiday, called *Purim Katan* (Little Purim). This is the story of one holiday, celebrated by the Jews of Frankfurt, Germany.

It began in 1614, when the Emperor Matthias decided to hold his coronation in the city. Most townspeople were excited by the news, but the head of the baker's guild had a different opinion. All he could think of was how to use the coronation to rid Frankfurt of its Jews. "They must be expelled," he told the city council, "or else the bakers will not allow the coronation to proceed. Either Frankfurt will have no Jews, or it will have no cake."

Most people were upset by this. The Jews were good customers and honest shopkeepers. Finally, the council decided not to expel the Jews but not to interfere with the baker's friends either.

The attack came on the very next day. Shops were looted and people were beaten up in the street. The riots lasted a long time, and many Jews decided to leave. In a few weeks, there were hardly any Jews left in Frankfurt.

Soon even Emperor Matthias knew what was happening in Frankfurt. He expected most of the expenses for his coronation to be paid for with a special tax on the Jewish community. Suddenly, there were no Jews, so there was no money. Furious, he ordered the baker to appear before him. "How dare you?" he shouted, "You think that you were bothering the Jews but, in fact, you were taking money from me." Nothing the baker said could calm the emperor. "You have stolen from

me and you will be punished severely." As the baker and his henchmen were taken away, they heard the Emperor summon his clerks. "Invite the Jews to return to Frankfurt. They are honest citizens and they should live there in peace."

The Emperor signed this proclamation on the twentieth day of the month of Adar, just six days after Purim. Every year since then, the Jews of Frankfurt celebrated that day as a second Purim, in honor of Emperor Matthias and how he saved them from the baker.

# פסח

## PESACH

עֲבָדִים
הָיִינוּ
לְפַרְעֹה
בְּמִצְרַיִם
וַיּוֹצִיאֵנוּ
ה׳ אֱלֹהֵינוּ
מִשָּׁם בְּיָד
חֲזָקָה
וּבִזְרֹעַ
נְטוּיָה.
ההגדה

We were slaves to Pharaoh in Egypt
and God took us out of there with a
strong hand and an outstretched arm.

*The Haggadah*

# WHAT IS.... PESACH

**I**t may still be cold and snowy in some places, but everywhere there are signs that spring is on the way. The snow is finally melting and the trees are growing new leaves. Here and there a patch of bright green grass is poking through the snow. Everywhere life is beginning anew. This is the perfect time for a holiday: we even call it *Chag Ha'Aviv*, the Holiday of Spring.

## HISTORY

**F**or hundreds of years, the Jews were slaves in Egypt. They worked very hard and were treated very cruelly, until one day, Moshe came along. Although he was born to a Jewish family, he was raised as an Egyptian prince and knew exactly how to speak to the Pharaoh and his advisers. "Let my people go!" he demanded, but the Egyptians wouldn't listen. It took ten plagues before Pharaoh finally begged Moshe to take the Jews out of Egypt. During these plagues, the Jews were spared - God passed over them and punished only the Egyptians. In Hebrew the word for passing over is *pasach*, and the holiday that celebrates how God passed over the Jews is called Pesach.

## THE LAND

**F**orty years after the Jews left Egypt, they finally made it to Israel, the Promised Land. They still celebrated Pesach every spring, but now Pesach became important for another reason. For the many Jews who now worked as farmers, Pesach was the season when their crops first started to bloom. This was the season when they would harvest the first grain, which they would later bring to the Temple in Jerusalem and offer to God.

## CUSTOMS

**A**fter four hundred years, the Jews were finally free - another name for Pesach is *Zman Cheiruteinu*, the Time of Our Freedom. After so much suffering, it is no wonder that the Jews were in such a hurry to leave Egypt. They started to prepare dough so that they would have bread to eat on the way, but in their rush to leave they had no time to let the dough rise before baking, so they just carried it on their backs. The bread they finally made from this dough was flat and dry, almost like crackers. Every Pesach, Jews still eat this bread to remind them how their ancestors left Egypt in a hurry. We call the bread *matzah*, and another name for Pesach is *Chag Ha'Matzot*, the Holiday of Matzot.

Every year at the time the Jews left Egypt, they held a big celebration to remember everything that happened to them. Over the years, the celebration became very organized. There is a time to tell the story of what happened in Egypt, a time to eat special foods to remind us about what happened, and a time to sing holiday songs about the miracles that occurred or just for fun. In Hebrew the word for "organized" is *seder*, and the celebration that we have on the first two nights of Pesach (or one night in Israel) is called the seder. The book we read at the seder is called the Haggadah.

**Marcy:** Max, why are you lying under your bed?

**Max:** I'm cleaning my room for Pesach. This is where I keep my best stuff.

**Marcy:** Like this turkey feather?

**Max:** Eagle feather.

**Marcy:** And this candle?

**Max:** For reading in bed after lights out. My flashlight is broken.

**Marcy:** This bag?

**Max:** That's where I keep my extra-special stuff. Hmm, it's empty.

**Marcy:** You know what all these things are, don't you?

**Max:** Priceless treasures, fit for the Max Museum.

**Marcy:** No, the feather and candle. They're exactly what you need to look for <u>chametz</u> in the house. They're what we use for <u>bedikat chametz</u>. Then we put the chametz in a bag and <u>burn</u> it in the morning.

**Max:** You see, I told my mother I needed all this stuff.

## Chametz

There are many foods, called chametz, that we do not eat during Pesach. They include anything made with grain, like bread, cookies, cake, and beer. Some people won't even eat *kitniyot* - foods like rice, corn, peas, or peanuts, because they can be made into flour which might be confused with chametz. Not only is it forbidden to eat chametz during Pesach; it is even forbidden to own it or have it in the house, so people rinse and scrub everywhere to make sure that no chametz is left over.

## Bedikat Chametz

Even after people clean their houses for Pesach, they want to make sure they didn't miss anything. That's why on the night before Pesach, we make one last check of the whole house, to be sure that we didn't forget anywhere. *Bedikat chametz*, which means "checking for chametz," is this last check in every single room and in every nook and cranny.

## Feather and Candle

To make sure that we can see chametz hiding in the darkest corners of the house, we look for it by candlelight. Then we sweep up whatever is left with a feather, to make sure that no crumbs remain.

## Burn

On the morning before Pesach, we take whatever chametz we still have in the house and burn it. We then say that any chametz that we might have missed no longer belongs to us and is "like the dust of the earth."

**Max:** Now I know what a slave is!

**Marcy:** What do you mean?

**Max:** My parents decided to celebrate Pesach for the first time. Last night I had to clean my room, and now I have to set the table for the seder.

**Marcy:** I know what you mean. I had to polish all the silverware, yuck! But my mother said that I can set up the seder plate after that.

**Max:** You know how to do that? Can you help us with it?

**Marcy:** Sorry, I won't have time today, but if you check at the bottom of the page there's a picture with all the seder foods: karpas, maror, charoset, zro'a, and an egg.

**Max:** And matzah.

**Marcy:** That goes underneath the seder plate.

**Max:** Thanks. Uh oh, I have to run. I hear my mother calling me again.

**Marcy:** Just remember, tonight we'll be free again.

## Seder Plate

In the middle of the seder table is a plate containing all the special foods that we eat during the seder.

## Karpas

We eat a piece of green vegetable dipped in salt water to remind us that Pesach marks the beginning of spring. The salt water tastes like the tears shed by our ancestors, in Egypt.

## Zro'a

The shank bone is the only item on the seder plate that we do not eat. It reminds us of the *Korban Pesach* (Pesach sacrifice).

## Maror

Maror, or bitter herbs, reminds us of the bitterness of slavery in Egypt. Most people use lettuce or horseradish (*chazeret*) for maror.

## Charoset

A mixture of chopped apples or dates, nuts, cinnamon, and wine, which reminds us of the mortar that the Jews used to build with when they were slaves. We sweeten the bitter maror by dipping it in charoset.

## Egg

The egg on the seder plate reminds us of the *Chagigah*, or additional holiday sacrifice that was offered in the Temple on Pesach. A hard-boiled egg is also a symbol of mourning for the Temple. Even in happy times, we must always remember the sad events of the past.

## Matzah

Matzah reminds us of the bread eaten by the Jews when they left Egypt, and of the stale bread that they ate when they were still slaves.

**Marcy:** I'm so happy you and your family have come to our house for the <u>second seder</u>.

**Max:** So am I. I spent the whole day memorizing the <u>Mah Nishtanah</u> and I want everyone to hear me.

**Marcy:** That's good. Last night my little brother was supposed to say it, but he got mixed up, and said Mah nishma instead.

**Max:** I know all four questions by heart. I even have a couple of my own.

**Marcy:** Me too. You are supposed to ask as many questions as you can during the seder. That way we can talk about all the miracles that happened when the Jews left Egypt.

**Max:** You mean we spend the whole seder talking about it? My mother always warns me not to talk with my mouth full.

**Marcy:** She's right. First we talk and then we eat. Look, my father's pouring the wine for <u>kiddush</u>. Get your <u>Haggadah</u>, and we'll go to the table.

**Max:** You just answered my first question.

**Marcy:** What was that?

**Max:** When do we start?

## Second Seder

Almost everywhere in the world we celebrate two seders - one on the first night and one on the second night of Pesach. In Israel, there is just one seder, on the first night, and then there is an extra day of Chol HaMo'ed, just like on Sukkot.

## Mah Nishtanah

Even the youngest children are encouraged to participate in the seder. In fact, everything at the seder is planned so that they stay interested and ask lots of questions. That's why the seder begins with the youngest child asking four questions about the seder: Why are we eating matzah instead of bread? Why are we eating strange vegetables? We are we dipping our food in salt water and charoset? Why are we leaning to the side instead of sitting up straight? These questions are called the Mah Nishtanah, which means "Why is this night different from any other night?" The adults answer them: *Avadim hayinu l'Pharaoh b'Mitzrayim*, "We were slaves to Pharaoh in Egypt," and then tell the story of how the Jews became free.

## Kiddush

Like on Shabbat and the other holidays, we begin the seder with kiddush over wine or grape juice. Throughout the evening we drink three more cups of wine, to show how happy we are to be free.

## Haggadah

The Haggadah is the book that tells the story of how the Jews were saved from Egypt. It contains many legends and songs, and sometimes even pictures, showing what happened when the Jews left Egypt. Some families read every word in the Haggadah. Others use it as a guide for telling the story of the Exodus. There are even some people who add their own prayers and poems to the Haggadah, to make it especially relevant to them.

# The Pesach Sandwich

Rabbi Levi Yitzchak's neighbor had a son who did not want to keep mitzvot. One year, during the seder, as the family was about to make a sandwich of matzah and maror for "korech," the boy pulled from his pocket two slices of bread and some meat, and made himself a sandwich. "How dare you bring bread to my seder?" his father shouted.

"But father," the boy answered, "I'm hungry. What difference does it make if I eat bread or matzah? I'm sure Rabbi Levi Yitzchak wouldn't mind." The father jumped up from the table and grabbed him. "Oh no? Let's ask him." The whole family marched next door, the father leading the boy by the ear. "Rabbi," the man said, "even you would not tolerate what my son just did. He ate bread at our seder. I have four sons, rabbi, and I don't have to tell you which one he is."

Everyone in the room was shocked; everyone, that is, except for Rabbi Levi Yitzchak. He smiled at the boy and asked if it was true.

"Of course, Rabbi. I was hungry so I made myself a sandwich."

"Don't you know that on Pesach, Jews don't eat bread," Rabbi Levi Yitzchak continued.

"Well, Rabbi," the boy answered, "to be totally honest, I don't really believe in all this. What difference could it possibly make if I eat bread or matzah?"

Everyone was silent. Only the boy's mother could be heard sobbing in the doorway. "Please come here," Rabbi Levi Yitzchak called to the boy. The boy walked slowly, afraid that this time he had gone too far. As he approached the table, the rabbi hugged him. "Such a fine boy," he said to the father, "and so honest too," he added to the mother. "He's ready to admit what he did and he's acting according to his beliefs. Such a fine, honest boy must sit with me at my seder. I have so much to learn from him! Just one thing, though..." The rabbi turned to the boy and said, "There'll be no sandwiches at our seder table - unless you make them with matzah."

**Max:** Asking all these questions makes me feel like one of the four sons - the wise one, of course! It's also making me feel really hungry.

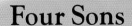

**Marcy:** Me too. Right now I could eat a horse.

**Max:** I could even eat maror.

**Marcy:** Soon you'll have a chance. First we have to eat matzah.

**Max:** What if I make myself a little matzah and maror sandwich?

**Marcy:** Good idea - but someone thought of it before you. We'll all eat matzah and maror sandwiches in a little while to remember what Hillel did at his seder two thousand years ago. He used to make a sandwich - korech - of matzah, maror, and the meat of the Korban Pesach.

**Max:** Very interesting, now can I have one of those sandwiches? I'm starving. And do you have anything to eat after the matzah and maror?

**Marcy:** We have a whole meal. And guess what we have for dessert.

**Max:** Matzah?

# Four Sons

In the Haggadah we tell the story of four sons who attended the seder. The wise son was like Max, who asked lots of questions and wanted to know everything. We are told to explain every last detail to him. The second son is bored and cynical: all he is asks is "Why do you do all these strange things?" We answer him sharply and say that this is why God took us out of Egypt. The third son is interested but he doesn't really know what's going on. The Haggadah says that we should explain the seder to him in a way that he can understand. The last son is too young to even ask any questions. We are told to encourage him to participate. No matter which son or daughter you are, everyone has a place at the seder.

# Korban Pesach

A long time ago, when the Temple was still standing, Jews everywhere would gather in Jerusalem for Pesach and bring a lamb as a sacrifice for the holiday. This lamb was called the Korban Pesach, and the meat from the lamb was roasted and eaten during the seder. The Korban Pesach reminds us of the lamb the Jews slaughtered in Egypt before they left. They took the blood of the lamb and painted their doorposts with it. Then, when God passed over Egypt during the plague of the firstborn, He saw the houses with the blood on the doorpost and spared the firstborn children living there.

**Marcy:** So where did you hide the <u>afikoman</u>?

**Max:** I'm not telling anyone until my parents promise to give me what I want.

**Marcy:** But you have to give it back. The afikoman is the last thing we eat during the seder.

**Max:** You can have a piece. but my parents know what they have to do first.

**Marcy:** Buy you a puppy?

**Max:** That's right. How do you know?

**Marcy:** I heard your mother tell my mother that they already bought you the puppy. You'll get it on Chol HaMo'ed.

**Max:** I will? Yes! La la la la la! I'm so happy I can sing! Dai-dai-einu.

**Marcy:** Hey. we sang that already. Now we're going to sing <u>Chad Gadya</u>.

**Max:** I have my own version now - one little puppy. one little puppy!

## Afikoman

The afikoman is the very last piece of matzah we eat at the seder, to remind us of the Korban Pesach. By now it is very late at night and the children are beginning to fall asleep. To keep them interested, we have a custom that the children steal the afikoman from their parents and hide it. They know that the seder can't go on without the afikoman, so they offer to give it back to their parents in exchange for a present that they will get during Chol HaMo'ed.

## Chad Gadya

Another way to keep children interested in the seder is to sing all their favorite songs at the end. One song we sing is *L'Shanah HaBa'ah BiYerushalayim*, Next Year in Jerusalem. Even though we were saved from Egypt, the Jewish People will never really be free until everyone is able to celebrate the holidays in Jerusalem. Perhaps the most popular song, though, is Chad Gadya, which tells the story of a little goat and what happened to it.

הקדוש
ברוך
הוא

**Max:** Marcy, what are you counting on your fingers?

**Marcy:** It's the Omer. I'm counting the days until Shavuot. There are only forty-three left.

**Max:** You really like these holidays, don't you? It's still Pesach, and you're already counting down to the next holiday.

**Marcy:** We're supposed to count, seven weeks from when we left Egypt till the day we received the Torah.

**Max:** You mean we have a holiday for seven weeks. That's great!

**Marcy:** Actually it's not such a happy time. During the Omer, the 24,000 students of Rabbi Akiva died, so, some Jews won't go to concerts, or even shave or get a haircut during the Omer.

**Max:** Okay, I promise I won't shave during the Omer either.

## Counting the Days

We count the days between two important dates in Jewish history - from the second night of Pesach, when we first became a free people after leaving Egypt, all the way to Shavuot, when we received the Torah.

## Omer

When the Temple was still standing, the Jews brought their first fruits as an offering to God during the seven weeks between Pesach and Shavuot. This was a very tense period for the farmers of Israel, who were only now finding out how their crops had grown. That's why, during the forty nine days of the Omer, they would not hold any celebrations like weddings or parties.

## Haircut

Much later, the Omer became a time of mourning for Rabbi Akiva's students who died during a revolt against Rome. There is still a custom of keeping some laws of mourning during most of the Omer.

# Flour for Pesach

It happened in Jerusalem in 1915 - the "Year of the Great Drought." There was no grain in the entire city. Pesach was only days away, and the Jews of Jerusalem wondered whether they would have matzot for the holiday.

Rabbi Yisrael, the leader of the Jewish community, was walking on the outskirts of town, when he noticed a cloud of dust winding toward the city. It was a caravan of camels. "Halloo there," he called to it. Soon an Arab merchant rode up to him. He looked worn and tired, but from his clothing, Rabbi Yisrael knew that he was quite wealthy.

"*Salaam Aleikum*," the merchant greeted him, "Is this the road to Damascus?"

"No," Rabbi Yisrael answered, "To Jerusalem. What a magnificent caravan."

"Magnificent?" he snorted, "It's only trouble. I've been carrying flour for weeks, but no one buys it. I just want to get home."

"Flour?" Rabbi Yisrael answered, "I would gladly buy it all, only I don't have the money. Our holiday of Pesach is just three days away and we need flour to bake matzah."

"Maybe we can help each other," the merchant suggested. "What if I give you the flour now, and you pay me back when I return in a month." Rabbi Yisrael agreed, and the Jews of Jerusalem had matzah for Pesach. During Chol HaMo'ed Rabbi Yisrael collected enough money to pay for all the flour, but the merchant never showed up, so he put the money in a bank. Years went by, but the merchant never returned. The sum in the bank doubled and tripled, but no one could touch it because it belonged to the Arab merchant.

Before he died, Rabbi Yisrael told his son what to do: "Wait ten more years. If the merchant comes back, you must pay him. If he doesn't, you must take the money and share it among the poor people of Jerusalem. This way, everyone will benefit from the merchant's kindness."

Ten years later, Rabbi Yisrael's son took some of the money to buy food and clothing for the poor people of Jerusalem. He did that before every holiday for many years.

# Yom HaSho'ah VehaGevurah

The Jewish People have known many tragedies throughout their history, but the Holocaust stands out clearly in the minds of everyone.

In the 1930s, Adolf Hitler, the German leader, set out to conquer the world and rid it of all the Jews. In Europe, where more Jews lived than anywhere else, he almost succeeded. Everywhere Hitler's Nazi regime reached, Jews were persecuted and forced into slave labor. Some fought back, like in the Warsaw Ghetto, but they had little chance against the powerful German army, which had overrun most of Europe. Others met their death in enormous concentration camps, like Auschwitz, or in death camps, like Treblinka.

Hitler ruled Germany for just twelve years; World War II was waged for only six. But in that time over six million Jews were shot, gassed, burned and tortured to death by the Nazis and their allies. One and a half million of these victims were children.

# The Gift of Life

Rochele looked at her baby brother, sleeping in her mother's arms. He had been crying all night, but then again everyone on the train was crying - even Papa. They had been traveling almost two days now. Rochele was tired and cold and very hungry.

all she could think about was the day the soldiers arrived in her town just a few months ago. Since then, she hadn't gone to school. Papa had a hard time

finding work, and last week her family barely celebrated her birthday. There was no party, no cake, just a small chocolate bar for a present. Her chocolate bar! It was on the bottom of her knapsack. Now, at least, she wouldn't be hungry.

Suddenly Rochele heard a faint cry: "Help me, somebody please help me," an old woman moaned. "Sshh!" Rochele whispered, "you'll wake up my brother." The old woman just kept on moaning.

She looked so feeble that Rochele knew she had to help. "Here," she said, giving her the chocolate, "it's all I have."

The woman smiled. "Let's share it," she said, taking half, "you also have to be strong." When they

62

finished eating, the woman slipped a tiny object into her hand. Even in the dark train, Rochele could see that it was a diamond ring. "Take it," she begged her, and Rochele knew that she couldn't refuse.

An hour later the train stopped and the doors squeaked open. Soldiers were shouting: "*Raus, raus*, everybody out!" Rochele's family rushed into the dirty train station. She saw hundreds of people, all of them Jews (she knew because of the yellow stars they wore). In a minute she saw a familiar face. Could it be Katya? No, Katya was the funniest girl she ever met, but this girl had such sad eyes. "Rochele!" the girl whispered. It was Katya! "Don't talk, I've been here a month and I know the routine. Whatever happens, stay on the right."

Soon, everyone was standing in a long line in front of a Nazi officer. Most of the people were being directed to the left. "To the right," Rochele thought, "to the right." When her family finally got there, Rochele and her father were sent to the right, but her mother and baby brother were sent to the left. "Please," Rochele pleaded, "let them go to the right!" The soldier grabbed her, but Rochele just took his hand and put the ring in it. The soldier paused for a moment: "Send the lady and baby with the girl!"

"I was that baby "And that's how your Great-Aunt Rochele saved my life," Grandpa finished the story.

Since Yom HaSho'ah is a quite recent event, there are few customs that have taken root everywhere to commemorate this very sad day. In Israel a siren is sounded. In some communities there are touching memorial services, in which people sing songs recalling the Sho'ah and read poems and personal accounts by people who lived through it. Sometimes survivors describe their experiences, while often people take turns reading the names of some of the victims. It is impossible to read all the names; there are so many that it would take years and years. It would be like reading the phone book dozens of times or naming all the people in your city or province. At most services, the people also recite the Yizkor prayer commemorating the dead, or the Kaddish. There may be slides or brief films, describing the events that took place, or simple artwork by children giving their own impressions of the Holocaust.

Only time will tell how Yom HaSho'ah will be observed in the future. All that is certain is that it will be observed. As a great Jewish scholar and survivor of the Holocaust said: "As Jews, we now have an additional commandment - 'Never Forget.'"

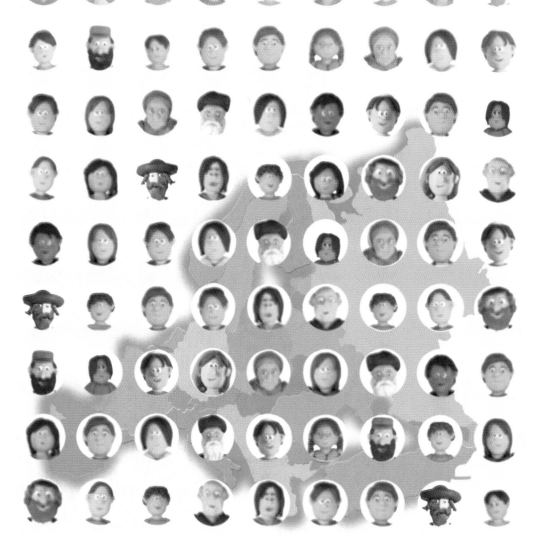

Here, along this map of Europe, are faces representing Hitler's victims.

Old and young, men and women, boys and girls, all died at Hitler's hands. Only a handful remained to rebuild Jewish life in Europe, America, and Israel. Imagine the victims as the black and white faces on the page, and the survivors as the colored faces.

# יום העצמאות
# יום הזיכרון

צוּר יִשְׂרָאֵל
וְגוֹאֲלוֹ, בָּרֵךְ
אֶת-מְדִינַת-
יִשְׂרָאֵל, רֵאשִׁית
צְמִיחַת גְּאֻלָּתֵנוּ.
הסידור

# YOM HA'ATZMA'UT  YOM HAZIKARON

Rock and Savior of Israel, bless the State of Israel, the beginning of our redemption

*The Siddur*

# WHAT IS.....YOM HA'ATZMA'UT

Most of the holidays we've celebrated until now were based on events that took place long ago. In fact, until 1948, the newest holiday we had was Chanukah. Finally, after two thousand years of exile, the Jews once again became an independent people in their own homeland. The day we regained our independence is Yom Ha'Atzma'ut. The day before we celebrate Yom Ha'Atzma'ut we observe Yom HaZikaron. On this day we remember the many people who died in the struggle to regain and keep our independence.

## HISTORY

During the long exile, Jews never lost hope that one day they would return to their country. Every day, in their prayers and celebrations, they would mention Israel and Zion. Often small groups of Jews would risk the dangerous journey to visit and settle in the land of Israel. About 100 years ago, a man named Theodor Herzl began promoting the idea that the Jews should have a country of their own. To create this country, Herzl founded the Zionist Movement. He traveled widely, convincing people of his ideas. Many of them eventually settled in Israel, where they rebuilt the ancient cities and even founded new ones. For the first time in two thousand years, there was a Jewish community in Israel of farmers, factory workers, doctors and lawyers. There were soldiers, policemen, firemen and clerks. The Jews in Israel came from Russia, America, Germany, Morocco, South Africa and even from China. They came from practically every corner of the world. On November 29, 1947, the United Nations voted to create a Jewish state in the Land of Israel, and in May 1948 the State of Israel was born.

## THE LAND

During the day of Yom Ha'Atzma'ut people go on picnics and visit the country's parks and gardens. Just take a deep breath - if you smell a barbecue, you know that somewhere nearby people are celebrating Yom Ha'Atzma'ut.

## CUSTOMS

Walking down the streets of Israel on Yom Ha'Atzma'ut you can see thousands and thousands of flags. There are flags hanging from buildings and homes, flags waving from lamp posts, and flags fluttering from passing cars. But the best time to walk down the street is at night. Bands play music and people dance in the streets, celebrating their independence.

**Max:** Marcy, can I have your beret?

**Marcy:** Sorry Max. I can't give it to you. My cousin Rina sent it to me. She just went into the army.

**Max:** What does she do in the army?

**Marcy:** She teaches parachuting.

**Max:** Isn't that dangerous?

**Marcy:** Of course it can be. That's why we want peace. Do you know that tomorrow is Yom HaZikaron, a special memorial day for all the soldiers who were killed in Israel's wars.

**Max:** I thought tomorrow was Yom Ha'Atzma'ut, Israel's Independence Day.

**Marcy:** No, that's in two days. On the day before Yom Ha'Atzma'ut, they hold special ceremonies in all the military cemeteries, like in Mount Herzl. They also have a siren, in the morning and the evening. When people hear the siren, everything comes to a stop, even the cars and the factories.

**Max:** Now I really need to have that beret.

**Marcy:** Okay, take it. I'll get my own beret in a few years when I join the army.

# Yom HaZikaron

There were many struggles along the way to creating a Jewish state. The Arab states along Israel's borders were not interested in having a new Jewish state near them. As soon as David Ben Gurion, Israel's first prime minister, declared Israel's independence in 1948, they attacked the new country. After a long war, the Jews were able to keep their independence, but only at great cost. Six thousand young Jewish men and women died during the War of Independence so that the Jewish People could once again be free. Since that time many more have died in wars with Israel's neighbors. That is why, on the day before Yom Ha'Atzma'ut, we have a special day, Yom HaZikaron, Remembrance Day, to remember all the soldiers and civilians who gave their lives for the country.

# Mount Herzl

Herzl never lived to see Israel become an independent state. He died at a very young age, after organizing several Zionist Congresses. After the first Zionist Congress in 1897, he wrote in his diary "In Basle I founded the Jewish State... In five years perhaps, and certainly in fifty, everyone will see it." He was right. In May 1948, the Jewish State was born. Once Israel became independent, Herzl's bones were reburied on the top of a mountain overlooking Jerusalem, the capital of the country he helped create. Surrounding him are the tombs of many of Israel's leaders and of the soldiers who died to keep Israel independent.

# Siren

The siren sounds twice in Israel on Yom HaZikaron, in the morning and in the evening. As soon as everyone hears the siren, the entire country comes to a stop. Cars stop, people stop, and everyone stands up to honor those who fell to protect the country.

**Max:** Marcy, can you help me with my homework?

**Marcy:** What homework? We didn't get any homework.

**Max:** I did. Because tomorrow is Yom Ha'Atzma'ut, we're going to surprise all the kids in the class who are making <u>aliyah</u> with good-bye presents. I want to surprise you.

**Marcy:** Thank you. How are you going to surprise me?

**Max:** I'm drawing your picture. What color are your eyes?

**Marcy:** Blue.

**Max:** Great, because all I have is a blue crayon. Don't move for a minute while I draw you.

**Marcy:** Can I take a look? Hey, I don't have three arms and I definitely don't have antennae! I have a better idea. Since we're having a Yom Ha'Atzma'ut party, and you've got a blue crayon, why don't you make me an Israeli <u>flag</u>?

**Max:** That's a great idea. Won't you be surprised!

## Flag

When Israelis decided to design a flag for their new state, someone pointed out that the Jews already had a flag, the tallit, which religious Jews wear every day when they pray. The white shawl with black or blue stripes on both sides would make a perfect flag. It was then decided to add a Magen David, the Star of David, which had long been a Jewish symbol, and in a few minutes, the Jews had a flag: a blue and white tallit with a blue Magen David.

## Aliyah

Just like an aliyah in the synagogue means going up to the Torah, whenever Jews move to Israel, it is called going on aliyah, or going up. Israel is a country of *olim* (immigrants, or people who went up) from practically every country in the world.

**Max:** Marcy, why are you limping?

**Marcy:** You're asking me why? Do you remember how many times you stepped on my feet?

**Max:** Sorry. I never danced the <u>hora</u> before. I never did any of that stuff before. I never even tried those Israeli meatballs.

**Marcy:** Those weren't meatballs. They were <u>falafel.</u>

**Max:** They must have <u>Hebrew</u> words for everything. Why can't people speak English like me?

**Marcy:** That's how they communicate. How else would people from America understand people from Russia, or Morocco, or Ethiopia?

**Max:** You mean you're going to have to speak Hebrew when you go to Israel too?

**Marcy:** I sure am.

**Max:** Then you better send me very simple letters. My Hebrew isn't that good yet.

# Hora

One of the most popular dances in Israel is the hora. Everyone stands in a circle and holds hands. Then they spin around, faster and faster, taking two steps to the right and kicking to the left.

# Falafel

Fried balls of chickpeas served with salad in pita bread and topped with sesame sauce. One of the few foods we didn't bring with us from Russia, Poland, Morocco or India, falafel is a local Palestinian delicacy that we gladly borrowed. Everywhere in Israel there are little stands with people selling falafel.

# Hebrew

When Jews started returning to Israel a hundred years ago, they found that they could not understand each other. Some spoke Russian or Yiddish while others spoke Arabic or Spanish. In Jerusalem alone, Jews spoke over twenty languages.

Some people thought that everyone should speak Hebrew, which they knew from their prayers and studies, but others thought that Hebrew was impractical. After all, no one had spoken it for thousands of years. "How can you ask for a cup of tea with two spoons of sugar when there are no words in Hebrew for tea, spoon or sugar," they'd ask.

One man, Eliezer Ben-Yehudah, refused to be discouraged. He searched through all the books he could find for Hebrew words that had been forgotten, and wrote them down in his dictionary. When there were no words, he simply made them up. He also insisted that his son, Itamar, be spoken to only in Hebrew. For many years Itamar was not allowed to go to school or even play with children who could not speak Hebrew. At first people thought Ben-Yehudah was insane. But he would not give up, and in a few years a number of other families also began speaking Hebrew at home. Within just forty years, Hebrew had become the official language of the Jews of the British Mandate of Palestine.

# The Flag

It happened only a few years ago, during the Lebanon War. Israeli tanks were chasing away the terrorists who threatened her northern boundary. A few tanks had gone too far, though, and rode right into an ambush. The tanks were destroyed, but many of their crews managed to escape. They were trapped in Lebanon, behind enemy lines, and all they knew was that their buddies were miles to the south. That night they began their long walk to safety.

They walked all night and hid all day. Although they didn't know the countryside, they couldn't stop anyone to ask directions. Instead they just followed their instincts, believing that they would eventually get home.

The journey was difficult: by the third night the men just plodded on. Finally, as the sun began to rise, someone noticed an Israeli flag in the distance. "The base!" he shouted, "we made it!"

From far away a guard at the base heard the distant shouting. He quickly radioed his commander with the news. "Terrorists," he warned, "only a mile north of us." Within seconds the base was on alert and guns were aimed at the approaching soldiers.

The soldiers stood up and began to run, when suddenly a bullet whizzed over their heads. "Duck!" they called to one another, "they think we're terrorists." The bullets got closer and closer, and shells were exploding just meters away, when one of the soldiers had an idea. "We know this is an Israeli base because of the flag," he thought. "Why don't we just show them our own flag?" He pulled off his knapsack and reached inside. At the bottom was his tallit, with a thick blue stripe on either side. He tied his tallit to the barrel of his rifle, and began waving it like a flag. The wind was blowing and the tallit began to flutter.

Looking at the scene through his binoculars, the commander of the base realized what was happening. "Stop shooting!" he barked into the radio, "*Hem mishelanu!* They're ours!"

Ever since then, on the anniversary of that day, the crew gets together and celebrates a holiday in honor of the tallit-flag that saved their lives.

וּסְפַרְתֶּם לָכֶם מִמָּחֳרַת הַשַּׁבָּת
מִיּוֹם הֲבִיאֲכֶם אֶת-עֹמֶר
הַתְּנוּפָה שֶׁבַע שַׁבָּתוֹת תְּמִימֹת תִּהְיֶינָה. ויקרא כ"ג ט"ו

# LAG BA'OMER

And you shall count for yourselves from the day after the day of rest on
which you brought the Omer, seven full weeks.

*Vayikra* 23:15

**Marcy:** Where have you been? Are you ready for the bonfire?

**Max:** Sorry I'm late. My mother made me get a haircut for Lag Ba'Omer. Here's my bow and arrows. I even brought you an apple. Put it on your head and see how well I can shoot.

**Marcy:** No way!

**Max:** Come on. Marcy. Isn't that what Bar Kochba did?

**Marcy:** Don't you know anything about Bar Kochba or Shimon Bar Yochai?

**Max:** I know about Bar Kochba because I peeked at the next page. I never heard about the other guy.

**Marcy:** He was one of the Rabbis who taught secretly - sometimes in caves - because the Romans forbade Jewish studies. The students took bows and arrows with them to their studies. That way. if they were seen by the Romans. they could say they were going hunting.

**Max:** That's amazing. I look for excuses to get out of school and they had to find excuses to get in!

## Lag Ba'Omer

For many Jews, the Omer is a sad time, recalling the thousands of students of Rabbi Akiva, who died during the Jewish Revolt against the Romans (132-135C.E.). Some Jews will not get married during the Omer or even listen to music or have a haircut. According to this tradition, Lag Ba'Omer, the 33rd day of the Omer, marks the day when the students stopped dying. Many people get married on this day and many have haircuts, to show that the period of mourning is over.

## Bar Kochba

Lag Ba'Omer also celebrates the revolt of Shimo Bar Kochba against the Romans, 64 years after th Temple was destroyed. Bar Kochba's revo eventually ended in failure. He died in battle alon with thousands of his followers. But for many Jew Bar Kochba is a great hero, who gave them hop after the Temple was destroyed and taught them to struggle again even the greatest odds to maintain their independence and identit Hundreds of years later, Jews in modern Israel regarded Bar Kochb as an inspiration in their fight to win Israel's independence.

## Shimon Bar Yochai

Shimon Bar Yochai, a scholar and mystic who lived at the same time as Bar Kochba, is another Jewish hero, who we remember on Lag Ba'Omer. According to the legend, some friends were discussing whether the Romans did any good when they ruled over Israel. One said that the Romans built roads and market places. But Shimon Bar Yochai responded that they built roads so that their soldiers could move freely and markets to sell their wares. When the Roman governor heard about this, he ordered that Bar Yochai be arrested. Bar Yochai fled to the mountains with his son, and hid in a cave for twelve years. The story says that during that time Bar Yochai learned many secrets of the Torah. In Israel today, thousands of people visit the tomb of Rabbi Shimon Bar Yochai on Mount Meron every Lag Ba'Omer, the anniversary of his death. They spend the night singing, dancing, and studying the Zohar, a book of Torah secrets.

# Little Yosef

Yosef hated being laughed at, especially by his older brother Daniel. So what if he was only thirteen. He could fight as well as any of them in Bar Kochba's army. "Hey Yosef!" Daniel called to him, "I thought I told you to go home. Don't you know what it takes to be in Bar Kochba's army?" Yosef knew exactly what it took. He heard about the men on horseback who had to pull a tree out by its roots while galloping by. He couldn't do that, but maybe there was still something he could do to help Bar Kochba.

There he was! Bar Kochba himself! Yosef blushed, imagining that Bar Kochba was staring at him. "And

who might you be?" Bar Kochba was staring at him. Yosef stared back and said in the deepest voice he could find: "I want to be in your army. I want to throw the Romans out of the country." Bar Kochba laughed. "You are brave. Maybe I can make a fighter out of you after all."

That was three years ago. Yosef spent two years carrying Bar Kochba's weapons before he was finally allowed to fight, but soon everyone knew about Yosef HaKatan, Little Yosef. "Little Yosef does big things," Bar Kochba used to laugh.

Now the war was over. Bar Kochba was dead. Daniel was dead. Beitar had fallen. Julius Severus, the great Roman general, wanted to meet Yosef and hear his story of the battle. The general was shocked to see that Yosef was only a boy. "This is the best soldier you could find among the survivors? You mean to say that I nearly lost to a child?" Yosef looked at him and remembered how Bar Kochba spoke to him just three years

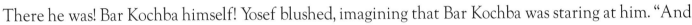

ago. "General" he stammered, "according to your custom, you will write to the Emperor, telling him that the war is over and that you and your troops are well. I may be a child but I know that is a lie. The war may be over, but neither you nor your troops are well." The general stared at him. "Do you know

who I am?" he asked. "Julius Severus," Yosef answered. "And you dare speak to me like this?" Yosef looked at him for a second and gathered his courage. "I lost my family, I lost my friends, I lost my country. What more can you take from me?" Julius Severus smiled. "Thank you," he said. "Now I know why I almost lost to a child."

That night, in his letter to the Emperor, Julius Severus crossed out the line saying that he and his troops were well. Yosef had taught him a lesson.

# The Archbishop and the Bonfire

It happened a long time ago in Spain, during the Inquisition. Although Jews were forbidden to keep their religion, many continued to secretly observe whatever customs they could. Because it was so difficult to keep Pesach, some Jews made an extra effort to observe Lag Ba'Omer. Even if they were caught, they could say that were just going on a family picnic. That's just what the de Aguilar family did.

That day, at sunset, Pedro de Aguilar and his family loaded up the donkey with wood and an enormous picnic supper and set out to a quiet spot in the forest. They even took little Juanita with this time - she was only eight years old and did not need to risk her life to celebrate Lag Ba'Omer. But she had cried, "Take me with to Lag Ba'Omer!" until her parents agreed to bring her along. They

didn't realize that some of the servants were suspicious, especially Pepe, a crafty boy who had overheard Juanita's crying: "If the de Aguilars are arrested," he thought, "maybe the Inquisition will reward me and give me all their property." Pepe often informed Archbishop Ramirez about the de Aguilar's strange behavior.

This time, though, Archbishop Ramirez was upset that Pepe came to bother him in the middle of dinner. He had heard of Pesach, he had heard of Yom Kippur, but he had never heard of Lag Ba'Omer. Still, he thought he should check it out for himself.

It was pitch black in the forest and the de Aguilars were enjoying their supper around the Lag Ba'Omer bonfire. Suddenly they heard the sound of horses in

the distance! "Quiet everyone," Pedro de Aguilar ordered. "Miguel, go and see who's coming." But before his son could go, Archbishop Ramirez appeared, along with Pepe and soldiers armed with muskets. "*Buenas noches*," began the Archbishop. "I hear you are having a little party, a Lag Ba'Omer party, as a matter of fact."

Pedro began to stammer an answer: "*Buenas*

noches, Archbishop Ramirez..." but before he could get any further, Juanita ran over to the Archbishop. "*Buenas noches, Señor* Archbishop. You always talk so funny, you make me laugh. What kind of party did you say we were having, Gagalomer?" Pedro's eyes lit up. Juanita had given him an idea.

"That's right, Archbishop, an Omer party. When we were Jews, the Omer was a sad time. For forty-nine days, we would not sing or dance or even take a haircut. We've been Christians for almost fifteen years now, and I thought it would be a good idea to celebrate the Omer happily, with a picnic."

"How wonderful," the archbishop smiled. "Do you mind if I join you?"

The next year all the Jews in town joined the de Aguilars at their Lag Ba'Omer bonfire. After all, even the archbishop received an invitation.

# WHAT IS..... YOM YERUSHALAYIM

After the Jews regained their independence in 1948, the city of Jerusalem was divided between Israel and Jordan, with much of the city, including the holy sites, out of reach to Israelis. All this changed in June 1967. For a long time, Israel's Arab neighbors had been threatening to destroy the country and it looked like they could. On June 5th, a war broke out, and in only six days the Israeli army ended the Arab threat, entered the old city of Jerusalem and reunited it with the rest of the city. The reunification is celebrated on 28th of Iyar - Yom Yerushalayim. The Arab-Israel conflict is not yet over, but the search for peace is underway. One meaning of the name Jerusalem is "City of Peace" and we hope and pray that one day all the people of Jerusalem will live in peace.

## City of Peace

According to the prophet Yishayahu, Jerusalem is the city where all the people of the world will come to worship God together. Until we can all live together in peace, Jerusalem will not be able to fulfill this very important role.

A wealthy Jew once came to visit his rabbi, who lived in another town in abject poverty. When the Jew entered the rabbi's room he saw nothing but a bed, a chair and a table - ill-constructed at that. He asked the rabbi why he lived in such poverty. Surely the visitor and other hassidim could help the rabbi to live a more comfortable life.

The rabbi asked his visitor where he was staying while in town, and the visitor gave the name of a small local hotel. "And what is in your room please?" asked the rabbi. "A bed, a chair and a table," answered the visitor. "And at home, where you live, what do you have?" "Fine French furniture, silver candlesticks, the best porcelain, beautiful linen..."

"And so it is with me," said the rabbi. "In my real home I have all the luxuries you could imagine, but here in my temporary dwelling I need very little." "And where is your real home?" asked the visitor. "In Jerusalem, where we all have a place to live," was the answer.

# שבועות

## SHAVUOT

וְלָקַחְתָּ מֵרֵאשִׁית כָּל־פְּרִי הָאֲדָמָה אֲשֶׁר תָּבִיא מֵאַרְצְךָ... וְשַׂמְתָּ בַטֶּנֶא וְהָלַכְתָּ אֶל־הַמָּקוֹם אֲשֶׁר יִבְחַר ה' אֱלֹהֶיךָ לְשַׁכֵּן שְׁמוֹ שָׁם.

דברים כ"ו ב

And you shall take the first fruits of the earth that shall come from your land... and you shall put them in a basket, and you shall go to the place where God will choose to dwell.

*D'varim 26:2*

# WHAT IS.....SHAVUOT

**W**hat does it mean to be free? Does it mean that you can do anything you want? Or does it mean that you have extra responsibilities just because you're free. This is one of the big issues that surround the holiday of Shavuot. Seven weeks ago was Pesach, when we celebrated gaining our freedom from Egypt. With that freedom also came responsibilities, and that means keeping the law and acting in a responsible manner. No people can survive their independence without laws to guide them and help them develop. That's why we celebrate Shavuot: to remind us that even free people have responsibilities.

# HISTORY

**F**or seven weeks after leaving Egypt the Jews wandered in the desert. They were heading to Israel, where they would have their own country. But before they could get there, they had to have their own laws. Even free people shouldn't lie or steal or forget their past. So, seven weeks after the Jews left Egypt, they gathered around Mount Sinai to receive the Torah, the book of laws that would tell them how to live.

**A**fter seven weeks (the word *Shavuot* means "weeks") the Jewish people stood around Mount Sinai and God spoke to them: "Do not worship idols. Remember the Sabbath. Honor your parents. Do not kill. Do not steal. Do not lie. Do not become jealous of your neighbors." When they heard these commandments, the Jews promised to obey them. For seven weeks the Jews had been a free people. Now they had a constitution to prove it.

# THE LAND

**I**t took the Jews forty years before they finally reached Israel and settled there. Most of them became farmers, and their most important crop was wheat, which they ground and baked into bread. They would begin to harvest their wheat before Shavuot. When the Temple was built, they brought their first sheaves of wheat there and offered them to God. They called this bringing *bikurim*, the first crops, and the journey to Jerusalem became a beautiful procession. Every town would pile its first crop - by now it included fruits and vegetables - on a wagon, pulled by two bulls. The wagons and the bulls would be decorated with flowers and gold and, of course, with fruits and vegetables that they had harvested. The people who led the wagon would sing and dance; some would play flutes and drums as they marched to Jerusalem to bring their fruits and grain to the Temple.

# CUSTOMS

**O**nce the Temple was destroyed, people no longer brought bikurim, and Shavuot celebrations focused more on the giving of the Torah on Mount Sinai. Many new customs emerged, like eating dairy foods. Shavuot is a summer holiday, and in the summer, people often eat light dairy foods. The Torah also gives many restrictions about eating meat. Some Jews say that since the Torah was not yet given, they ate only dairy foods, for which there are very few restrictions.

**A**nother custom that developed over the years is to stay up all night and study Torah. According to one legend, the night before the Jews received the Torah on Mount Sinai, everyone got a good night's sleep. When God saw this, He was disappointed. "I would have thought that they would be so excited that they couldn't fall asleep." Many Jews now stay up all night and study on Shavuot, to show how excited they really are about receiving the Torah.

**Max:** Why are you bringing <u>flowers</u> to school? You must really like the teacher!

**Marcy:** They're for Shavuot. We're going to decorate the classroom with them. Look at the photograph I've brought to put on the wall.

**Max:** What's that – a vegetable market?

**Marcy:** No, that's my pen pal, Ruth, on her kibbutz in Israel.

**Max:** Is that an eggplant hanging from her ceiling?

**Marcy:** Yes, and look at those bundles of wheat Ruth's holding!

**Max:** So what is she going to do? Make bread?

**Marcy:** Don't be silly! She's going to be the star of the <u>bikurim</u> pageant, like in the days of the Temple in Jerusalem! Except now they take the crops to the center of the kibbutz. Then everyone sings and dances and performs plays to celebrate Shavuot. Can you guess who she is?

**Max:** Little Red Riding Hood?

**Marcy:** No, she's <u>Ruth</u> from the Bible.

**Max:** I knew that.

## Flowers

One popular custom on Shavuot is to decorate homes and synagogues with flowers and leaves to show that nature is blossoming. According to one legend, when the Torah was given even Mount Sinai in the middle of the desert was covered with grass and flowers.

## Bikurim

In Israel today, the custom of bringing bikurim has been revived, particularly in the kibbutzim and moshavim. After almost two thousand years, bringing bikurim again plays a major role in the Shavuot celebrations

## Ruth

The Book of Ruth tells the story of a young widow, who moved with her mother-in-law Naomi to Bethlehem, and married Boaz, a local leader and a relative of her late husband. Many Jews read the Book of Ruth in the synagogue on Shavuot. The story centers around the harvest season, which takes place during Shavuot. It also describes how Ruth, who was born in Moab, chose to become part of the Jewish people by accepting the commandments - in fact, she was to become an ancestor of King David. This provides another reason as to why we read the Book of Ruth. By joining the Jewish people, Ruth accepted the Torah, just like the tradition says all Jews did at Mount Sinai on Shavuot. The Book of Ruth teaches us that, with devotion and commitment, anyone can become a prominent member of the Jewish People.

# Ami's Garden

Ami wanted to be a farmer, just like the grown-ups on his kibbutz. It was a new kibbutz, and they could certainly use all the help they could get, and besides, Ami was the only child on the kibbutz, so he had no one to play with. His parents didn't understand this, though. "You're too young," they said, "maybe in a few more years. Until then there are plenty of chores for you."

One day, as Ami finished feeding the chickens, he noticed that he still had some grain left over. "Why don't I take this grain and plant my own field, where nobody can see it," he thought. In a few minutes he was in his secret place, a little valley not far from the kibbutz. Using a stick, he dug a furrow and placed the seeds inside. Then he watered his plants, with the water in his canteen.

That night at dinner, everyone ate watermelon. Ami saved his seeds so that he could plant them. In fact, almost every day he planted something new, and his garden was beginning to grow. Of course, he told no one about it. He wanted to wait until just before Shavuot, when everything could be harvested. Only now the grown-ups were so busy with their own crops that no one had time for Ami. "Oh well," he thought, "I'll surprise everyone during bikurim."

One afternoon, Ami smelled smoke coming from the direction of the fields. Soon he heard shouting, too. A brush fire had broken out and was burning up all the crops. By the time he got there to help put the fire out, it was too late. All the crops were destroyed.

The next morning, the kibbutz held a meeting. "Tomorrow is Shavuot," Ami's father began, "and we were hoping to bring bikurim from our own crops. Unfortunately, the fire destroyed everything, and it will take a long time before we will have any produce of our own."

Ami suddenly jumped up. "But we do have crops, Abba." Everyone stared at him. "I grew them myself. When you told me I was too young to work in the

fields, I planted my own garden."

Ami's father took his hand. "Do you want to take us there, Ami?"

"Yes, Abba," and he led the whole kibbutz to his secret place. Nobody could believe what they saw. There were tomatoes, watermelons, eggplants, cucumbers, and even a little patch of wheat, all ready to be harvested.

The next day the kibbutz invited all the neighboring kibbutzim to come see their bikurim parade. Everyone dressed in their best clothes and carried baskets filled with crops from Ami's little garden. At the head of the parade was Ami, of course. After all, he had grown everything himself.

**Max:** It's great that we don't have to go to sleep tonight. What should we play first?

**Marcy:** What do you mean play? We're going to study all night.

**Max:** Study all night?!

**Marcy:** It's the custom on the night of Shavuot. We make up for the night we slept instead of preparing ourselves to receive the Torah.

**Max:** But I didn't sleep - I wasn't even there!

**Marcy:** Well, you were, sort of! Every Jew stood at Mount Sinai in spirit, when God offered us the Torah. Do you know what we said? Na'aseh v'Nishma - we will do and we will listen.

**Max:** Wow! So I was also at Mount Sinai. Wait till I tell Stanley. He's never even been out of the city.

## Study All Night

Some people have a custom to spend the whole night of Shavuot studying the Torah. One custom is to read a special book called *Tikun Leil Shavuot*, which contains extracts from all the books of the Torah and the Talmud. That way, people who read the Tikun have learned a little bit about every book in the Torah.

## Na'aseh V'Nishma

This famous answer reflects the way Jews throughout history related to the Torah. Even if they couldn't understand the logic behind the commandments and customs, they were ready to follow them without question.

**Max:** I know that today is <u>Shiv'ah Asar B'Tammuz</u>. I know that it's a fast day. I know that we are supposed to mourn the destruction of Jerusalem. But look at this postcard - Jerusalem seems like a pretty nice place to me.

**Marcy:** Well it was destroyed thousands of years ago. It's been rebuilt since.

**Max:** Aha! So why are people still so upset?

**Marcy:** Well, maybe because Jerusalem isn't fully rebuilt yet, because there is still war in the world and Jerusalem is supposed to be the city of peace. Maybe it's just good to <u>remember</u> the sad things that happened long ago. That way we can make sure they never happen again.

# Shiv'ah Asar B'Tammuz

The seventeenth of Tammuz is a sad day in the Jewish calendar. It is the anniversary of the day in 70 C.E. when the Roman armies broke through the walls of Jerusalem during their war against the Jews. Three weeks later they destroyed the Temple, and the Jews were sent into exile. According to tradition, many other tragedies occurred on the seventeenth of Tammuz. For example, the Mishnah says that Moshe came down from Mount Sinai on this day, carrying the Ten Commandments. When he saw people worshiping the Golden Calf, he became so angry that he broke the stone tablets on which the commandments were written. It would take another eighty days for Moshe to go back up the mountain and receive the commandments again.

# Remember

Even in the happiest times, it is important to remember the sad events of the past. At Jewish weddings, for example, the groom usually breaks a glass, to show that even on the happiest day of his life, he still remembers the destruction of Jerusalem, two thousand years ago. As a philosopher said not too long ago: "Those who forget the past are condemned to repeat it."

**Marcy:** Max. why do you look so angry?

**Max:** It's Stanley. He really makes me mad. He won't come swimming with me! He won't go to the movies either. What kind of a friend is that?

**Marcy:** Maybe he doesn't want to because it's the Nine Days.

**Max:** Oh yeah? That's what he says. Well. I'm still angry at him because he just quit our soccer team to play with the big kids. I hate those guys.

**Marcy:** I think you have a bad case of sinat chinam.

**Max:** No. I just forgot my handkerchief. I have allergies, you know.

**Marcy:** That's not what I mean. Sinat chinam is hating people for no reason. Some people say that Jerusalem was destroyed because of sinat chinam.

**Max:** No way. It was destroyed because of Babylonians and Romans. I listened during school, not like Stanley. Hey, there he is! Sorry, Marcy, can't stop to talk. We're late for soccer practice!

# The Nine Days

The days before Tisha B'Av are a very solemn time. Some Jews won't eat meat or go swimming or to the movies. Others use this time to remember how, and more importantly, why Jerusalem and the Temple were destroyed in the first place - because people treated each other unkindly. They make an extra effort to try and help one another and show compassion for everyone they meet.

# Sinat Chinam

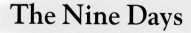

There's an ancient legend that describes why Jerusalem was destroyed. It all started over a misunderstanding...

A man decided to throw a party. He sent invitations to all the important people in Jerusalem and to his closest friend, Kamtza. Unfortunately, there was a mix-up, and the invitation that was supposed to go to Kamtza accidentally got sent to Bar Kamtza, who the man had hated for a very long time. Bar Kamtza was very excited to get the invitation. He thought that the man wanted to apologize and be his friend again. He jumped into the bath, got all dressed up, and ran to the party. But when he got there, the host cried: "What are you doing here? How dare you come to my house? Get out !" "Please," begged Bar Kamtza, "don't throw me out. I promise I won't even eat anything. Just don't embarrass me by throwing me out." The man refused to listen. In front of all the guests, he had his servants carry Bar Kamtza out. Bar Kamtza fumed. "How dare he! And not one guest was willing to stick up for me. I'll teach them."

Instead of going home, he went straight to the Roman governor of Jerusalem. "Your Excellency," he began, "the Jews of Jerusalem are planning a revolt." He told a long story to trick the governor into believing that it was true. The governor massed his armies, laid siege to Jerusalem, and eventually destroyed the city - because two people hated each other.

**Marcy:** Are you still angry with Stanley? You really look upset.

**Max:** Of course I'm upset. Today is my birthday and I can't even have a party because it's <u>Tisha B'Av</u>. Instead of having a party, all I did was <u>sit on the floor</u> and read the Book of <u>Eichah</u>. No party, no cake, no presents!

**Marcy:** But you're so lucky!

**Max:** How am I lucky? Didn't you hear what I just said?

**Marcy:** I did, but did you know that there's an old Jewish legend that the <u>Messiah</u> will be born on Tisha B'Av.

**Max:** Really?

**Marcy:** And did you know that he will be called Menachem, the Comforter?

**Max:** My Hebrew name is Menachem!

**Marcy:** I don't know, Max. There may be more to you than meets the eye!

**Max:** I always said that.

# Eichah

The Book of Eichah, written, according to tradition, by the prophet Yirmiyahu, is a poetic description of the destruction of Jerusalem and the First Temple by the Babylonians in 586 B.C.E.

# Tisha B'Av

Tisha B'Av is a day of commemoration of some of the most tragic events in Jewish history. Both Temples were destroyed on Tisha B'Av and the Jews were expelled from Spain on Tisha B'Av.

# Messiah

Even in their saddest moments, Jews have always tried to find a glimmer of hope for a better future. That's why there is an ancient Jewish legend that the Messiah will be born on Tisha B'Av, and that a solution lies within every difficulty. According to this legend, the Messiah will be called Menachem, the Comforter, because he will bring peace and comfort to the world. The legend ends by saying that Tisha B'Av, now the saddest day in the Jewish calendar, will one day become a very happy holiday.

# Sit on the Floor

When Jews mourn, there is a custom to sit on the floor rather than on chairs to show that we cannot be comfortable in our sadness.

# Remembering Jerusalem

It was fourteen years since Akiva had seen his wife. He had been away studying, just as she had wanted, and he was now the famous Rabbi Akiva, with thousands of students. Only he knew that he would still be a simple

shepherd if his wife hadn't encouraged him to study. He felt in his pocket for the present he had bought her. Good, it was still there. Now the question was when to surprise her with it. It would probably be best when they were alone. After dinner they would go for a walk and then he would give it to her. He also knew exactly where they would go for a walk.

Rachel was surprised that Akiva chose to walk with her on the ruins of Jerusalem. She hadn't been there in so many years, since she was a child and Jerusalem was a great city. She knew the city well then, and almost everyone in it. Her father, Kalba Savua, was once the richest man in the city. He was a kind man, who gave food and money to anyone in need. Some people said that even a dog would come away from his house with a full belly.

But Jerusalem was destroyed by the Romans, and all that was left were a few charred stones. She cried as she passed by the ruins of what was once her home. Rabbi Akiva didn't notice though. He was just happy finally to be back with his wife. As they walked past where the Temple once stood, a fox darted out in front of them. Rachel remembered the Temple well - better even than her husband, who probably never saw it from up close . Still, it annoyed her that he was actually laughing at the fox. "How can you laugh," she complained, "After fourteen years, don't you know that this is where the Temple once stood?"

Rabbi Akiva smiled and put his arm around her. "I do," he answered, "and just as the prophets said that foxes will play in the Temple's courtyards, they also said that Jerusalem will be rebuilt one day. I see that one prophecy has already come true. Why should I doubt that the other one will come true too?" Rachel looked at her husband and understood why everyone said he was the wisest rabbi in the land. He looked at her and continued: "Until then, I have something to remind you of

Jerusalem." He reached into his pocket and pulled out a gold tiara, shaped like the walls of the city. "Every time you wear this, remember the fox we saw tonight, and remember that Jerusalem will be rebuilt, too."

"That promise is the greatest gift you can give me," she said, as they walked down the hill to their home.

**Marcy:** What do you think of my new dress?

**Max:** It's okay. Why are you so fancy?

**Marcy:** Have you forgotten? It's my goodbye party. I borrowed this dress especially for it.

**Max:** Oh, right, of course I remember. But I'm not going to dance. Do you want me to step on your feet again. Last time you limped for a week.

**Marcy:** But Max, it's Tu B'Av. I'm going to have to risk it. They even decorated the gym to look like a vineyard. All the boys are going to hide while the girls start dancing.

**Max:** Hide and seek, eh? This is getting interesting.

**Marcy:** And then the boys will pop out and find partners to dance with.

**Max:** And what if I stay hidden?

**Marcy:** Then you'll miss the food.

**Max:** Okay, I'll go. Just make sure you wear your heavy boots, in case I step on your feet again.

**Marcy:** I'm already wearing them!

## Borrowed

Sometimes boys would only want to marry a pretty girl or a rich girl. They would forget that what is really important is not how pretty the girl is or how rich her family is, but how kind and caring a person she is. To remind the boys of this, the girls would sing a verse from the Book of Mishlei: *Sheker ha'chen v'hevel hayofi* (grace is deceptive and beauty, insignificant). They would also exchange clothing with one another so that the boys would not know who could really afford expensive dresses and who was only borrowing them.

## Dance

In ancient times, Tu B'Av was celebrated with enormous parties. All the girls would dress in white and gather in a vineyard to dance. While they were dancing, the boys would come and join them. Sometimes they would even fall in love as they danced away the night.

## Tu B'Av - the 15th of Av

One week after Tisha B'Av, one of the saddest day of the Jewish calendar, comes Tu B'Av, which is one of the happiest days. Tu B'Av marked the end of summer and of all the holidays for that year. In just a few weeks, Jews could look forward to the cycle of holidays starting again with Rosh HaShanah. For many centuries, the holiday of Tu B'Av was forgotten, but now many Jews are looking for ways to revive it.

**Max:** Hey, you're sitting in my seat.

**Sophie:** How could it be your seat if it's the first day of school?

**Max:** I sat here all of last year, right next to Marcy.

**Sophie:** I know Marcy. We just moved into her apartment. Her family moved to Israel.

**Max:** That's right. I just got a letter from her. She says she's been waking up at six o'clock every morning to go to <u>Selichot.</u>

**Sophie:** Selichot? Is that Hebrew for school?

**Max:** Nope! Beit-sefer is Hebrew for school. You're new here, aren't you?

**Sophie:** Yes. I've never been to Jewish school before. What's it like?

**Max:** Boy, have you got a lot to learn. The same thing happened to me last year.

**Sophie:** So there's lots to do here.

**Max:** Lot's of things to do here and at home – it's not homework though and, well, why don't we just go back to page 2?

**Sophie:** What about page 1?

**Max:** Naaah, that's for parents and teachers.

## Selichot

During the week before Rosh HaShanah many Jews wake up early to say special prayers asking for forgiveness (*selichah* in Hebrew) for all the mistakes they made over the past year. In Jerusalem, where Marcy lives, people wake up at dawn to begin the day by saying how sorry they are for all the mistakes they made, and how they will try to behave better in the coming year.

## Go back to page 2

Like the Jewish year, this book never really ends. It just goes right back to the beginning . . . Shanah Tovah!

## Other products from Scopus Films:

### The Shabbat Book
Stories, songs, texts & anecdotes - A weekly guide for the whole family

### Shalom Shabbat Video
Songs, stories & clay animation with Chaim Topol, Hanny Nahmias

### Shalom Shabbat Audiocassette
Shabbat songs to sing with family & friends

### The Animated Haggadah
Book, Video, Activity Book, CD-ROM

### The Animated Menorah
Book & Activity Book

### Megillat Esther
Illustrated scroll & Activity Book

### Shirim K'tanim
Series of eight videos - Hebrew songs for children

### The Shirim K'tanim Song Festival
One-hour video compilation with English presenter

### Fliegel's Flight
A video bird's-eye view of Jewish history

Available from:
### Lambda Publishers Inc.
3709 13th Ave., Brooklyn, NY 11218, USA
Tel: (718)972-5449 | Fax: (718)972-6307 | e-mail: animatedjewishyear@ejudaica.com
www.lambdapublishers.com | www.UrimPublications.com